Applied Regression and Modeling

Applied Regression and Modeling

A Computer Integrated Approach

Amar Sahay

Applied Regression and Modeling: A Computer Integrated Approach

First published in 2016 by
Business Expert Press, LLC
222 East 46th Street, New York, NY 10017
www.businessexpertpress.com

ISBN-13: 978-1-63157-329-3 (paperback)
ISBN-13: 978-1-63157-330-9 (e-book)

Business Expert Press Quantitative Approaches to Decision Making Collection

Collection ISSN: 2163-9515 (print)
Collection ISSN: 2163-9582 (electronic)

Cover and interior design by Exeter Premedia Services Private Ltd., Chennai, India

First edition: 2016

10 9 8 7 6 5 4 3 2 1

Printed in the United States of America.

Abstract

Applied Regression and Modeling: A Computer Integrated Approach creates a balance between the theory, practical applications, and computer implementation behind Regression—one of the most widely used techniques in analyzing and solving real world problems. The book begins with a thorough explanation of prerequisite knowledge with a discussion of Simple Regression Analysis including the computer applications. This is followed by Multiple Regression—a widely used tool to predict a response variable using two or more predictors. Since the analyses of regression models involve tedious and complex computations, complete computer analysis including the interpretation of multiple regression problems along with the model adequacy tests and residual analysis using widely used computer software are presented. The use of computers relieves the analyst of tedious, repetitive calculations, and allows one to focus on creating and interpreting successful models.

Finally, the book extends the concepts to Regression and Modeling. Different models that provide a good fit to a set of data and provide a good prediction of the response variable are discussed. Among models discussed are the nonlinear, higher order, and interaction models, including models with qualitative variables. Computer analysis and interpretation of computer results are presented with real world applications. We also discuss all subset regression and stepwise regression with applications. Several flow charts are presented to illustrate the concepts. The statistical concepts for regression, computer instructions for the software—Excel and MINITAB—used in the book and all of the data files used can be downloaded from the website link provided.

Keywords

coefficient of correlation, correlation, dependent variable, dummy variable, independent variable, interaction model, least squares estimates, least squares prediction equation, linear regression, multiple coefficient of determination, multiple regression and modeling, nonlinear models, regression line, residual analysis, scatterplot, second-order model, stepwise regression

Contents

Preface

This book is about regression and modeling—one of the most widely used techniques in analyzing and solving real-world problems. Regression analysis is used to investigate the relationship between two or more variables. Often we are interested in predicting one variable using one or more variables. For example, we might be interested in the relationship between two variables: sales and profit for a chain of stores, number of hours required to produce certain number of products, number of accidents versus blood alcohol level, advertising expenditures and sales, or the height of parents compared to their children. In all these cases, regression analysis can be applied to investigate the relationship between the variables.

The book is divided into three parts—(1) prerequisite to regression analysis followed by a discussion on simple regression, (2) multiple regression analysis with applications, and (3) regression and modeling including second-order models, nonlinear regression, regression using qualitative or dummy variables, and interaction models in regressions. All these sections provide examples with complete computer analysis and instructions commonly used in modeling and analyzing these problems. The book deals with detailed analysis and interpretation of computer results. This will help readers to appreciate the power of computer in applying regression models. The readers will find that the understanding of computer results is critical to implementing regression and modeling in real-world situation.

The purpose of simple regression analysis is to develop a statistical model that can be used to predict the value of a response or dependent variable using an independent variable. In a simple linear regression method, we study the linear relationship between two variables. For example, suppose that a Power Utility company is interested in developing a model that will enable them to predict the home heating cost based on the size of homes in two of the Western states that they serve. This model involves two variables: the heating cost and the size of the homes.

The first part of the book shows how to model and analyze this type of problem.

In the second part of the book, we expand the concept of simple regression to include multiple regression analysis. A multiple linear regression involves *one dependent or response* variable, and *two or more independent variables* or *predictors*. The concepts of simple regression discussed in the previous chapter are also applicable to the multiple regression. We provide graphical analysis known as matrix plots that are very useful in analyzing multiple regression problems. A complete computer analysis including the interpretation of multiple regression problems along with the model adequacy tests and residual analysis using a computer are presented.

In the third part of the book, we discuss different types of models using regression analysis. By model building, we mean selecting the model that will provide a good fit to a set of data, and the one that will provide a good prediction of the response or the dependent variable. In experimental situations, we often encounter both the quantitative and qualitative variables. In the model building examples, we will show how to deal with qualitative independent variables. The model building part also discusses the nonlinear models including second-order, higher order, and interaction models. Complete computer analysis and interpretation of computer results are presented with real-world applications. We also explain how to model a regression problem using dummy variables. Finally, we discuss all subset regression and stepwise regression and their applications.

The book is written for juniors, seniors, and graduate students in business, MBAs, professional MBAs, and working people in business and industry. Managers, practitioners, professionals, quality professionals, quality engineers, and anyone involved in data analysis, business analytics, and quality and six sigma will find the book to be a valuable resource.

The book presents an in-depth treatment of regression and modeling in a concise form. The readers will find the book easy-to-read and comprehend. The book takes the approach of organizing and presenting the material in a way that allows the reader to understand the concepts easily. The use of computers in modeling and analyzing simple, multiple, and higher order regression problems is emphasized throughout the book. The book uses the most widely used computer software in data analysis and quality used in industry and academia. Readers interested in more complex and in-depth analysis of regression models are referred to additional resources that provides further details of the subject matter. In this book, we have provided numerous examples with data files, stepwise computer instructions, and case problems.

Acknowledgments

I would like to thank the reviewers who took the time to provide excellent insights which helped shape this book.

I would especially like to thank Mr. Karun Mehta, a friend and engineer. His expertise and tireless efforts in helping to prepare this text is greatly appreciated.

I am very thankful to Prof. Edward Engh for reviewing the book and providing thoughtful advice. Ed has been a wonderful friend and colleague. I have learned a great deal from him.

I would like to thank Dr. Roger Lee, a senior professor and colleague for reading the initial draft and administering invaluable advice and suggestions.

Thanks to all of my students for their input in making this book possible. They have helped me pursue a dream filled with lifelong learning. This book won't be a reality without them.

I am indebted to senior acquisitions editor, Scott Isenberg; director of production, Charlene Kronstedt; marketing manager; all the reviewers and collection editors, and the publishing team at Business Expert Press for their counsel and support during the preparation of this book. I also wish to thank Donald N. Stengel, Editor for reviewing the manuscript and providing many helpful suggestions for improvement. I acknowledge the help and support of Exeter Premedia Services—Chennai, India—Team for reviewing and editing the manuscript.

I would like to thank my parents who always emphasized the importance of what education brings to the world. Lastly, I would like to express a special appreciation to my wife Nilima, to my daughter Neha and her husband David, my daughter Smita, and my son Rajeev for their love, support and encouragement.

Computer Software Integration, Computer Instructions, and Data Files

We wrote the book so that it is not dependent on any particular software package; however, we have used the most widely used packages in regression analysis and modeling. We have also included the materials with the computer instructions in Appendix A of the book. The computer instructions are provided for both Excel and MINITAB that will facilitate using the book. Included are the following supplementary materials and data files in separate folders:

- Excel Data Files
- MINITAB Data Files
- APPENDIX_A: Computer Instructions for Excel and MINITAB
- APPENDIX_B: Statistical Concepts for Regression Analysis

All of the preceding materials can be downloaded from the Web using the following link:

URL: http://businessexpertpress.com/books/applied-regression-and-modeling-computer-integrated-approach

CHAPTER 1

Introduction to Regression and Correlation Analysis

Introduction

In real world, managers are always faced with massive amount of data involving several different variables. For example, they may have data on sales, advertising, or the demand for one of the several products his or her company markets. The data on each of these categories—sales, advertising, and demand is a variable. Any time we collect data on any entity, we call it a variable and statistics is used to study the variation in the data. Using statistical tools we can also extract relationships between different variables of interest. In dealing with different variables, often a question arises regarding the relationship between the variables being studied. In order to make effective decisions, it is important to know and understand how the variables in question are related. Sometimes, when faced with data having numerous variables, the decision-making process is even more complicated. The objective of this text is to explore the tools that will help the managers investigate the relationship between different variables. The relationships are critical to making effective decisions. They also help to predict one variable using the other variable or variables of interest.

The relationship between two or more variables is investigated using one of the most widely used tools—***regression and correlation analysis***. Regression analysis is used to study and explain the mathematical relationship between two or more variables. By mathematical relationship we mean whether the relationship between the variables is linear or nonlinear. Sometimes we may be interested in only two variables. For example, we may be interested in the relationship between sales and advertising. Companies spend millions of dollars in advertising and expect that an increase in the advertising expenditure will significantly improve the sales. Thus, these two variables are related. Other examples where two variables might be related are production cost and the volume of production, increase in summer temperature and the cooling cost, or the size of house in square-feet and its price. Once the relationship between two variables is explained, we can predict one of the variables using the other variable. For example, if we can establish a strong relationship between sales and advertising, we can predict the sales using advertising expenditure. This can be done using a mathematical relationship (to be explained later) between sales and advertising. There is another tool often used in conjunction with regression analysis known as **correlation analysis**. This correlation explains the degree of association between the two variables; that is, it explains how strong or weak the relationship between the two variables is.

The relationship between **two** variables is explained and studied using the technique of **simple regression analysis**. Managers are also faced with situations where many variables are involved. In such cases, they might be interested in the possible relationship between these variables. They may also be interested in predicting one variable using several variables. This problem is more involved and complex due to multiple variables involved. The problem involving many variables is studied using the technique of **multiple regression analysis**. Owing to the complex nature of multiple regression problems, computers are almost always used for this analysis.

The objective in simple regression is to predict one variable using the other. The variable to be predicted is known as the **dependent** or **response** variable and the other one is known as the **independent** variable or **predictor**. Thus, the problem of simple regression involves one dependent and one independent variable. An example would be to predict the sales (the dependent variable) using the advertising expenditure (the independent variable). In multiple regression problems, where the relationship between multiple variables is of interest, the objective is to predict one variable—the dependent variable using the other variables known as independent variables. An example of multiple regression would be to predict the sales for a grocery chain using the food-item sales, nonfood-item sales, size of the store, and the operating hours (12 or 24 hours). *The multiple regression problem involves one dependent and two or more independent variables.*

The problems of simple and multiple linear regressions assume that the relationship between the variables is ***linear***. This is the reason these are referred to as the ***simple linear regression*** and ***multiple linear regression***. It is important to note that the relationship between the variables is not always linear. Sometimes, a linear relationship between the variables may not exist. In such cases, the relationship between the variables can be best explained using a nonlinear relationship. By nonlinear relationships, we mean a curvilinear relationship that can be described using a quadratic or second-order or higher order equation. In analyzing such complex regression models, a computer package is almost always used. In this text, we have used Excel and MINITAB® computer packages to analyze the regression models. We have demonstrated the applications of simple, multiple, and higher order regressions using these software. The reason for using Excel is obvious. It is one of the most widely used spreadsheet programs in industry and academia. MINITAB is the leading statistical software for quality improvement and is used by 90% of Fortune 100 companies. It is also widely used as a teaching tool in colleges and universities. It is worth mentioning at this point that Excel is a spreadsheet program and was not designed for performing in-depth statistical analysis. It can be used for analyses up to a certain level but lacks the capability of producing in-depth reports for higher order regression models. If you perform regression analysis with substantial amount of data and need more detailed analyses, the use of statistical package such as MINITAB, SSS®, and SPSS® is recommended.

The statistical concepts needed for regression are included in **Appendix B**. This includes a review of statistical techniques that are necessary in explaining and building regression models. The graphical and numerical methods used in statistics and some more background information including the sampling, estimation and confidence intervals, and hypothesis testing are provided in **Appendix B**. The readers can download the Appendix at their convenience through a link provided. In the subsequent chapters of the book, we discuss and provide complete analysis (including computer analysis) and interpretation of simple and multiple regression analysis with applications; regression and modeling including second-order models, nonlinear regression, regression models using qualitative (dummy) variables, and interaction models. All these sections provide examples with complete computer analysis and interpretation of regression and modeling using real-world data and examples. The detailed analysis and interpretation of computer results using widely used software packages will help readers to gain an understanding of regression models and appreciate the power of computer in solving such problems. All the data files in both MINITAB and Excel formats are provided in separate folders. The step-wise computer instructions are provided in **Appendix A** of the book. The readers will find that the understanding of computer results is critical to implementing regression and modeling in real-world situations.

Before we describe the regression models and the statistical and mathematical basis behind them, we present some fundamental concepts and graphical techniques that are helpful in studying the relationships between the variables.

Measures of Association Between Two Quantitative Variables: The Scatterplot and the Coefficient of Correlation

Describing the relationship between two quantitative variables is called a ***bivariate relationship***. One way of investigating this relationship is to construct a ***scatterplot***. A scatterplot is a two-dimensional plot where one variable is plotted along the vertical axis and the other along the horizontal axis. The pairs of points (x_i, y_i) plotted on the scatterplot are helpful in *visually* examining the relationship between the two variables.

In a scatterplot, one of the variables is considered a *dependent variable* and the other an *independent variable*. The data value is thought of as having a (x, y) pair. Thus, we have (x_i, y_i), $i = 1, 2, \ldots, n$ pairs. One of the easiest ways to explain the relationship between the two variables is to plot the (x, y) pairs in the form of a scatterplot. Computer packages such as Excel and MINITAB provide several options for constructing scatterplots. Figure 1.1 shows a scatterplot depicting the relationship between sales and advertising expenditure for a company (***Data file: SALES&AD.MTW***).

From Figure 1.1, we can see a distinct increase in sales associated with the higher values of advertisement dollars. This is an indication of a

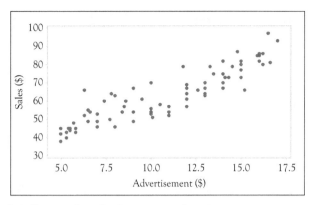

Figure 1.1 *Scatterplot of sales versus advertisement*

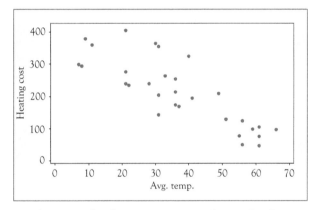

Figure 1.2 **A scatterplot depicting inverse relationship between heating cost and temperature**

positive relationship between the two variables where we can see a positive trend. This means that an increase in one variable leads to an increase in the other.

Figure 1.2 shows the relationship between the home heating cost and the average outside temperature (***Data File: HEAT.MTW***). This plot shows a tendency for the points to follow a straight line with a negative slope. This means that there is an *inverse or negative relationship* between the heating cost and the average temperature. As the average outside temperature increases, the home heating cost goes down. Figure 1.3 shows a weak or no relationship between quality rating and material cost of a product (***Data File RATING.MTW***).

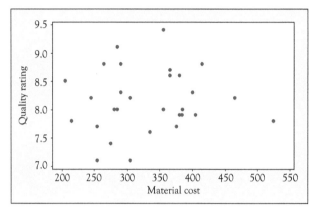

Figure 1.3 *Scatterplot of quality rating and material cost (weak or no relationship)*

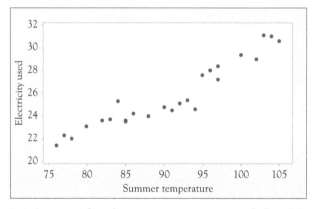

Figure 1.4 **A scatterplot of summer temperature and electricity used**

In Figure 1.4, we have plotted the summer temperature and the amount of electricity used (in millions of kilowatts) (**Data File: SCATTER1.MTW**). The plotted points in this figure can be well approximated by a straight line. Therefore, we can conclude that a linear relationship exists between the two variables.

The linear relationship can be explained by plotting a regression line over the scatterplot as shown in Figure 1.5. The equation of this line is used to describe the relationship between the two variables—temperature and electricity used.

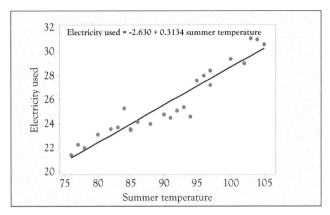

Figure 1.5 Scatterplot with regression line

These plots demonstrate the relationship between two variables visually. The plots are very helpful in explaining the types of relationship between the two variables and are usually the first step in studying such relationships. The regression line shown in Figure 1.5 is known as the line of "best fit." This is the best-fitting line through the data points and is uniquely determined using a mathematical technique known as the *least squares method*. We will explain the least squares method in detail in the subsequent chapters. In regression, the least squares method is used to determine the best-fitting line or curve through the data points in the scatterplot and provides the equation of the line or curve that is used in predicting the dependent variable. For example, the electricity used for a particular summer temperature in Figure 1.5 can be predicted using the equation of the line.

In these examples, we demonstrated some cases where the relationships between the two variables of interest were linear—positive or direct linear and inverse or negative linear. In a direct linear or positive relationship, the increase in the value of one variable leads to an increase in the other. An example of this was shown earlier using the sales and advertising expenditure for a company (Figure 1.1). The inverse relationship between the two variables shows that the increase in the value of one of the variables leads to a decrease in the value of the other. This was demonstrated in Figure 1.2, which shows that as the average outside temperature increases, the heating cost for homes decreases.

The *covariance* and *coefficient of correlation* are used to study the strength or degree of association between the two variables. Out of these two—the covariance has certain limitations. The coefficient of correlation is a better measure of degree of association between two variables and is widely used. The value of the correlation coefficient shows how strong the relationship between the two variables is. This is very important in the decision-making process, which involves making predictions. We will provide more details on these two measures in Chapter 2.

Scatterplot Showing a Nonlinear Relationship Between *x* and *y*

In many cases, the relationship between the two variables under study may be nonlinear. Figure 1.6 shows the plot of the yield of a chemical process at different temperatures (***Data File: YIELD.MTW)***. The scatterplot of the variables, temperature (*x*) and the yield (*y*) shows a nonlinear relationship that can be best approximated by a quadratic equation. The plot shows a strong relationship between *x* and *y*. The equation relating the temperature and the yield can be very useful in predicting the maximum yield or optimizing the yield of the process. The fitted curve along with the equation is shown in Figure 1.6. Usually a computer package is used to develop such relationship. The equation of the fitted curve in Figure 1.6 obtained using a computer package is $y = -1{,}022 + 320.3x - 1.054x^2$. The equation can

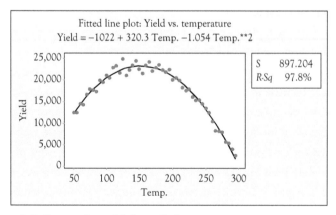

Figure 1.6 Scatterplot with best-fitting curve

be used to predict the yield (y) for a particular temperature (x). This is an example of nonlinear regression. The detailed analysis and explanation of such regression models will be discussed in subsequent chapters.

Matrix Plots

A matrix plot is a useful graphical tool to investigate the relationships between pairs of variables by creating an array of scatterplots. In regression analysis and modeling, often the relationship between multiple variables is of interest. In such cases, matrix plots can be created to visually investigate the relationship between the response variable and *each* of the independent variables or predictors. Matrix plots can also be created to display the relationship between the response variable and one or many independent variables simultaneously.

The visual displays in the form of matrix plots can show whether there is a linear or nonlinear relationship between the response and each of the independent variables or the predictors. They also display whether there is direct or indirect relationships between the response and the independent variables. This information obtained from the matrix plots is very helpful in building the correct model and prediction equation.

Figure 1.7 shows a matrix plot of the dependent variable—heating cost (y) with each of the independent variables: average temperature (x_1), house size (x_2), and age of the furnace (x_3).

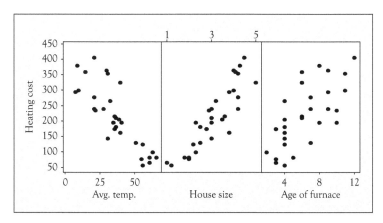

Figure 1.7 Matrix plot of heating cost (y) and each of the independent variable

The matrix plot in Figure 1.7 was developed using **each Y versus each X**. From this plot, it is evident that there is a negative relationship between the heating cost and the average temperature. This means that an increase in the average temperature leads to decreased heating cost. Similarly, the relationship between the heating cost and the other two independent variables—house size and age of the furnace is obvious from this matrix plot. Figure 1.8 shows another form of matrix plot depicting the relationship between the home heating cost based on the average outside temperature, size of the house (in thousands of square feet), and the life of the furnace (years) by creating an array of scatterplots.

Using Figure 1.8, the simultaneous effect of heating cost and the three independent variables can be assessed easily. The plot has three columns and three rows.

The first column and the first row in Figure 1.8 show the relationship between the heating cost (the response variable) and one of the independent variables, average temperature. The second row shows the relationship between the heating cost and two of the independent variables—the average temperature and the house size, while the third row in the plot shows the relationship between the heating cost and the three independent variables. The previous visual displays are very useful in studying the relationships among variables and creating the appropriate regression models.

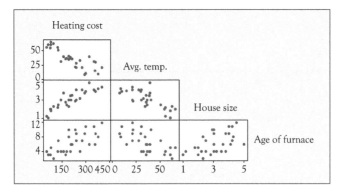

Figure 1.8 A matrix plot of average temp, house size, furnace age, and heating cost

Summary

This chapter introduced a class of decision-making tools known as ***regression and correlation analysis***. Regression models are widely used in the real world in explaining the relationship between two or more variables. The relationships among the variables in question are critical to making effective decisions. They also help to predict one variable using the other variable or variables of interest. Another tool often used in conjunction with regression analysis is known as ***correlation analysis***. The correlation explains the degree of association between the two variables; that is, it explains how strong or weak the relationship between the two variables is. The simplest form of regression explores the relationship between ***two*** variables and is studied using the technique of ***simple regression analysis***. The problem involving many variables is studied using the technique of ***multiple regression analysis***. The objective in simple regression is to predict one variable using the other. The variable to be predicted is known as the ***dependent*** or ***response*** variable and the other one is known as the ***independent*** variable or ***predictor***. *The multiple regression problem involves one dependent and two or more independent variables.* Describing the relationship between two quantitative variables is called a ***bivariate relationship***. The chapter also introduced and presented several *scatterplots and matrix plots. These plots are critical in investigating the* relationships between two or more variables and are very helpful in the initial stages of constructing the correct regression models. A computer software is almost always used in building and analyzing regression models. We introduced some of these widely used computer packages in this chapter.

CHAPTER 2

Regression, Covariance, and Coefficient of Correlation

This chapter provides an introduction of regression and correlation analysis. The techniques of regression enable us to explore the relationship between variables. We will discuss how to develop regression models that can be used to predict one variable using the other variable, or even multiple variables. We will explain the following features related to regression analysis: (1) Concepts of dependent or response variable and independent variables, or predictors; (2) the basics of the least squares method in regression analysis and its purpose in estimating the regression line; (3) determining the best-fitting line through the data points; (4) calculating the slope and y-intercept of the best-fitting regression line and interpreting the meaning of regression line; and (5) measures of association between two quantitative variables: the covariance and coefficient of correlation.

Linear Regression

Regression analysis is used to investigate the relationship between two or more variables. Often we are interested in predicting a variable y using one or more independent variables $x_1, x_2, \ldots x_k$. For example, we might be interested in the relationship between two variables: sales and profit for a chain of stores, number of hours required to produce a certain number of products, number of accidents versus blood alcohol level, advertising expenditures and sales, or the height of parents compared to their children. In all these cases, regression analysis can be applied to investigate the relationship between the two variables.

In general, we have one ***dependent*** or ***response*** variable, y, and one or more *independent variables*, $x_1, x_2, \ldots x_k$. The independent variables are also called **predictors**. If there is only one independent variable x that we are trying to relate to the dependent variable y, then this is a case of **simple regression**. On the other hand, if we have two or more independent variables that are related to a single response or dependent variable, then we have a case of multiple regression. In this section, we will discuss simple regression, or to be more specific, simple linear regression. This means that the relationship we obtain between the dependent or response variable y and the independent variable x will be linear. In this case, there is only one predictor or independent variable (x) of interest that will be used to predict the dependent variable (y).

In regression analysis, the dependent or response variable y is a random variable, whereas the independent variable or variables $x_1, x_2, \ldots x_k$ are measured with negligible errors and are controlled by the analyst. The relationship between the dependent and independent variable or variables are described by a mathematical model known as a **regression model**.

The purpose of simple regression analysis is to develop a statistical model that can be used to predict the value of a response or dependent variable using an independent variable.

The Regression Model

In a simple linear regression method, we study the linear relationship between two variables, the *dependent* or the *response variable* (y) and the *independent variable* or *predictor* (x). An example explaining the simple regression is presented as follows.

Suppose that the Mountain Power Utility company is interested in developing a model that will enable them to predict the home heating cost based on the size of homes in two of the Western states that they serve. This model involves two variables: the heating cost and the size of the homes. We will denote them by y and x, respectively. The manager in charge of developing the model believes that there is a positive relationship between x and y meaning that the larger homes (homes with larger square-footage) tend to have higher heating cost. The regression model relating the two variables—home heating cost y as the dependent variable and the size of the homes as the independent variable x—can be denoted using Equation 2.1. This equation shows the relationship between the values of x and y, or the independent and dependent variable and an error term in a simple regression model.

$$y = \beta_0 + \beta_1 x + \varepsilon \qquad (2.1)$$

where y = dependent variable x = independent variable

β_0 = y-intercept (population) β_1 = slope of the population regression line

ε = random error term (ε is the Greek letter "epsilon")

The model represented by Equation 2.1 can be viewed as a population model in which β_0 and β_1 are the parameters of the model. The error term ε represents the variability in y that cannot be explained by the relationship between x and y.

In our example, the population consists of all the homes in the region. This population consists of subpopulations of each home of size, x. Thus, one subpopulation may be viewed as all homes with 1,500 square feet, another consisting of all homes with 2,100 square feet, and so on. Each of these subpopulations consisting of size x will have a corresponding distribution of y values with the mean or expected value $E(y)$. The relationship between the expected value of y or $E(y)$ and x is the ***regression equation*** given by:

$$E(y) = \beta_0 + \beta_1 x \qquad (2.2)$$

where $E(y)$ = is the mean or expected value of y for a given value of x

β_0 = y-intercept of the regression line β_1 = slope of the regression line

The regression equation represented by Equation 2.2 is of a straight line describing the relationship between $E(y)$ and x. This relationship shown in Figure 2.1(a) to (c) can be described as positive, negative, or no relationship. The positive linear relationship is identified by a positive slope. It shows that an increase in the value of x causes an increase in the mean value of y or $E(y)$, whereas a negative linear relationship is identified by a negative slope and indicates that an increase in the value x causes a decrease in the mean value of y.

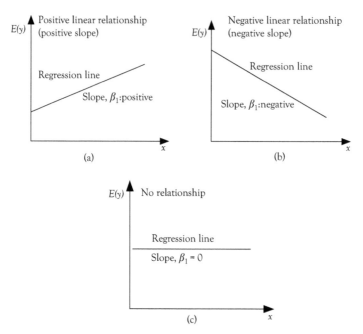

Figure 2.1 Possible linear relationship between E(y) and x in simple linear regression

The no relationship between x and y means that the mean value of y or $E(y)$ is the same for every value of x. In this case, the regression equation cannot be used to make a prediction because of a weak or no relationship between x and y.

The Estimated Equation of Regression Line

In Equation 2.2, β_0 and β_1 are the unknown population parameters that must be estimated using the sample data. The estimates of β_0 and β_1 are denoted by b_0 and b_1 that provide the **estimated regression equation** given by:

$$\hat{y} = b_0 + b_1 x \qquad (2.3)$$

where $\hat{y}$ = point estimator of $E(y)$ or the mean value of y for a given value of x

b_0 = y-intercept of the regression line b_1 = slope of the regression line

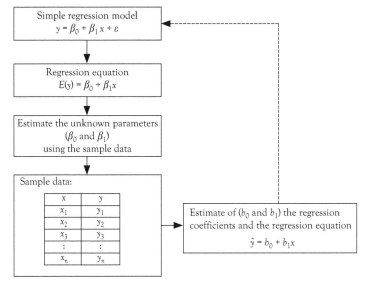

Figure 2.2 Estimating the regression equation

The preceding regression equation represents the estimated line of regression in the slope intercept form. The y-intercept b_0 and the slope b_1 in Equation 2.3 are determined using the **least squares method**. Before we discuss the least squares method in detail, we will describe the process of estimating the regression equation. Figure 2.2 explains this process.

The Method of Least Squares

The regression model is described in the form of a regression equation that is obtained using the **least squares method**. In a simple linear regression, the form of the regression equation is $y = b_0 + b_1 x$. This is the equation of a straight line in the slope intercept form.

We will illustrate the least squares method using an example. Suppose that the sales manager of a company is interested in the relationship between the advertising expenditures and sales. He has a good reason to believe that an increase in advertising dollars leads to increased sales. The manager has the sales and advertising data from 15 different regions shown in Table 2.1. To investigate the relationship between the sales and advertisement expenditures, a scatterplot was created that visually depicts the possible relationship between two variables.

Figure 2.3 shows a scatterplot of the data of Table 2.1 (**Data File: SALES & ADEXP**). Scatterplots are often used to investigate the relationship between two variables. An investigation of the plot shows a positive relationship between sales and advertising expenditures; therefore, the manager would like to predict the sales using the advertising expenditure using a simple regression model.

As outlined earlier, a simple regression model involves two variables where one variable is used to predict the other. The variable to be predicted is the dependent or response variable, and the other one is the independent variable. The dependent variable is usually denoted by y while the independent variable is denoted by x.

In a scatterplot the dependent variable (y) is plotted on the vertical axis and the independent variable (x) is plotted on the horizontal axis.

Table 2.1 Sales and advertisement data

Sales (y) ($1,000s)	Advertising (x) ($1,000s)
458	34
390	30
378	29
426	30
330	26
400	31
458	33
410	30
628	41
553	38
728	44
498	40
708	48
719	47
658	45

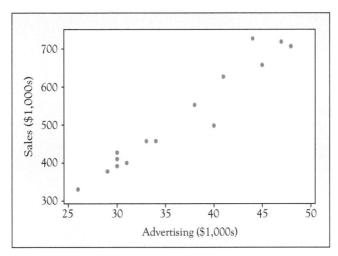

Figure 2.3 Scatterplot of sales and advertisement expenditures

The scatterplot in Figure 2.3 suggests a positive linear relationship between sales (y) and the advertising expenditures (x). From the figure, it can be seen that the plotted points can be well approximated by a straight line of the form $y = b_0 + b_1 x$ where, b_0 and b_1 are the y-intercept and the slope of the line. The process of estimating this regression equation uses a widely used mathematical tool known as the ***least squares method.***

The least squares method requires fitting a line through the data points so that the sum of the squares of errors or residuals is a minimum. These errors or residuals are the vertical distances of the points from the fitted line. Thus, the least squares method determines the best-fitting line through the data points that ensures that the sum of the squares of the vertical distances or deviations from the given points and the fitted line are a minimum.

Figure 2.4 shows the concept of the least squares method. The figure shows a line fitted to the scatterplot of Figure 2.3 using the least squares method. This line is the estimated line denoted using y-hat ($\hat{y}$). The equation of this line is given in the following. The method of estimating this line will be illustrated later.

$$\hat{y} = -150.9 + 18.33x$$

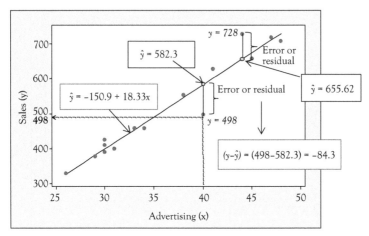

Figure 2.4 Fitting the regression line to the sales and advertising data of Table 2.1

The vertical distance of each point from the line is known as the *error or residual*. Note that the residual or error of a point can be positive, negative, or zero depending on whether the point is above, below, or on the fitted line. If the point is above the line, the error is positive, whereas if the point is below the fitted line, the error is negative.

Figure 2.4 graphically shows the errors for a few points. To demonstrate how the error or residual for a point is calculated, refer to the data in Table 2.1.

This table shows that for the advertising expenditure of 40 (or, $x = 40$) the sales is 498 or ($y = 498$). This is shown graphically in Figure 2.4. The estimated or predicted sales for $x = 40$ equals the vertical distance all the way up to the fitted regression line from $y = 498$. This predicted value can be determined using the equation of the fitted line as:

$$\hat{y} = -150.9 + 18.33x = -150.9 + 18.33(40) = 582.3$$

This is shown in Figure 2.4 as $\hat{y} = 582.3$. The difference between the observed sales, $y = 498$, and the predicted value of y is the error or residual and is equal to

$$(y - \hat{y}) = (498 - 582.3) = -84.3$$

The figure shows this error value. This error is negative because the point $y = 498$ lies below the fitted regression line.

Now, consider the advertising expenditure of $x = 44$. The observed sales for this value is 728 or $y = 728$ (from Table 2.1). The predicted sales for $x = 44$ equals the vertical distance from $y = 728$ to the fitted regression line. This value is calculated as:

$$\hat{y} = -150.9 + 18.33x = -150.9 + 18.33(44) = 655.62$$

The value is shown in Figure 2.4. The error for this point is the difference between the observed and the predicted value, which is:

$$(y - \hat{y}) = (728 - 655.62) = 72.38$$

This value of the error is positive because the point $y = 728$ lies above the fitted line.

The errors for the other observed values can be calculated in a similar way. The vertical deviation of a point from the fitted regression line represents the amount of error associated with that point. The least squares method determines the values b_0 and b_1 in the fitted regression line $\hat{y} = b_0 + b_1 x$ that will minimize the sum of the squares of the errors. Minimizing the sum of the squares of the errors provides a unique line through the data points such that the distance of each point from the fitted line is a minimum.

Since the least squares criteria require that the sum of the squares of the errors be minimized, we have the following relationship:

$$\sum (y - \hat{y})^2 = \sum (y - b_0 - b_1 x)^2 \tag{2.4}$$

where y is the observed value and $\hat{y}$ is the estimated value of the dependent variable given by $\hat{y} = b_0 + b_1 x$.

Equation 2.4 involves two unknowns, b_0 and b_1. Using differential calculus, the following two equations can be obtained:

$$\sum y = nb_0 + b_1 \sum x$$
$$\sum xy = b_0 \sum x + b_1 \sum x^2 \tag{2.5}$$

These equations are known as the ***normal equations*** and can be solved algebraically to obtain the unknown values of the slope and y-intercept b_0 and b_1. Solving these equations yields the results shown as follows.

$$b_1 = \frac{n\sum xy - \left(\sum x\right)\left(\sum y\right)}{n\sum x^2 - \left(\sum x\right)^2} \qquad (2.6)$$

and

$$b_0 = \frac{1}{n}\left(\sum y - b_1 \sum x\right) \text{ that can be written as}$$

$$b_0 = \bar{y} - b_1\bar{x} \text{ where} \qquad (2.7)$$

$$\bar{y} = \frac{\sum y}{n} \text{ and } \bar{x} = \frac{\sum x}{n}$$

The values b_0 and b_1 when calculated using Equations 2.6 and 2.7 minimize the sum of the squares of the vertical deviations or errors. These values can be calculated easily using the data points (x_i, y_i), which are the observed values of the independent and dependent variables (the collected data in Table 2.1).

Measures of Association Between Two Quantitative Variables: The Covariance and the Coefficient of Correlation

In the study of regression, the relationship between two or more quantitative variables is of interest. This relationship is described using scatterplots. These plots are very effective in describing such relationships visually. In a scatter plot, the pairs of points (x_i, y_i) plotted in order *visually* shows the relationship between the two variables. In this plot, a distinct increase in one variable (x-variable) resulting into an increase in the other variable (the y-variable) is an indication of a *positive relationship* between the two variables. On the other hand, an increase in one variable leading to a decrease in the other variable indicates a negative or inverse relationship. An example would be the relationship between the home heating

cost and the average outside temperature. As the average outside temperature increases, the home heating cost goes down.

In this section, we examine two measures of relationship between two
quantitative variables: the covariance and the coefficient of correlation.
The covariance has certain limitations; therefore, coefficient of correlation
is widely used to measure how strong the relationship is between two
variables.

The Covariance

The covariance is a measure of *strength* of linear relationship between two
quantitative variables x and y.

Example 2.1

We will calculate the covariance of the data in Table 2.1. This table
shows the advertising expenditures and the corresponding sales for
15 companies. Both the sales and advertising are in thousands of
dollars.

    a. Construct a scatterplot with sales on the vertical axis and advertis-
       ing on the horizontal axis. Comment on the relationship between
       the sales and advertising.

    b. Calculate the covariance and interpret the result.

Solution:

  (a) The scatterplot was shown earlier in Figure 2.3.

  (b) The covariance calculated using the following equation is:

$$s_{xy} = \frac{\sum (x_i - \bar{x})(y_i - \bar{y})}{n-1} = 978.586$$

Interpretation of Covariance

The positive value of S_{xy} indicates a positive linear relationship between
x and y. This means that as the value of x increases, the value of y also
increases. A negative value of S_{xy} is an indication of a negative linear

relationship between x and y. If the covariance is negative, the value of y decreases as the value of x increases. A value of S_{xy} close to zero indicates no or very weak relationship between x and y. The scatterplot in Figure 2.3 shows a positive relationship between x and y; that is, as the advertising expenditure (x) increases, the value of sales (y) also increases. This shows a positive covariance that is confirmed by the calculated value of $S_{xy} = 978.586$.

Limitation of Covariance

It should be noted that a large positive value of the covariance does not mean a strong positive linear relationship between x and y. Similarly, a large negative value of the covariance does not necessarily mean a strong negative linear relationship. *In fact, the value of the covariance is a quantity that depends on the units of measurement for x and y. For example, if x and y are measured in feet and then converted to inches, the covariance will show a much larger value for the values measured in inches.* This is a drawback of calculating the covariance. There is another measure of the relationship between two variables that is not affected by the units of measurement for x and y. This is known as **correlation coefficient or coefficient of correlation** and is discussed in the next section.

The Coefficient of Correlation

The sample coefficient of correlation (r_{xy}) is a measure of relative strength of a linear relationship between two quantitative variables. This is a unit less quantity. Unlike covariance, where the value depends on the units of measurements of x and y, the coefficient of correlation has a value between –1 and +1 where a value of –1 indicates a perfect negative correlation and a value of +1 indicates a perfect positive correlation. A perfect negative or positive correlation means that if the x and y values are plotted using a scatterplot, all the points will lie on a straight line. If the scatterplot shows a positive linear relationship between x and y the calculated coefficient of correlation will be positive, whereas a negative relationship between x and y on the scatterplot will provide a negative value of the coefficient of correlation.

Note that a value of correlation coefficient (r_{xy}) closer to +1 indicates a strong positive relationship between x and y, whereas a value of r_{xy} closer to −1 indicates a strong negative correlation between the two variables x and y. A value of r_{xy} that is zero or close to zero, indicates no or weak correlation between x and y.

Example 2.2: Calculating the Covariance and Coefficient of Correlation

Calculate the sample coefficient of correlation (r_{xy}) of the advertising and sales data (Table 2.1).

Solution: Often the covariance and coefficient of correlation (r_{xy}) can be calculated easily using a computer because of the complexity involved in manual calculations. The computer results are shown in Table 2.2.

Table 2.2 Covariance and correlation coefficient using MINITAB

Covariance: Sales (y), Advertising (x)		
	Sales (y)	Advertising (x)
Sales ($1,000)	19,032.410	
Advertising ($100)	**978.586**	53.400
Correlation: Sales (y), Advertising (x)		
Pearson correlation of Sales (y) and Advertising (x) = 0.971		
P-value = 0.000		

Note: The coefficient of correlation is also known as **Pearson correlation**. The coefficient of correlation is 0.971. This indicates a strong positive correlation between sales and advertising. The covariance of 978.586 is also an indication of positive covariance.

Examples of Coefficient of Correlation

Figure 2.5(a) through (d) shows several scatterplots with the correlation coefficient. Figure 2.5(a) shows a positive correlation between the profit and sales with a correlation coefficient value $r = +0.979$.

Figure 2.5(b) shows a positive relationship between the sales and advertisement expenditures with a calculated correlation coefficient, $r = +0.902$. Figure 2.5(c) shows a negative relationship between the

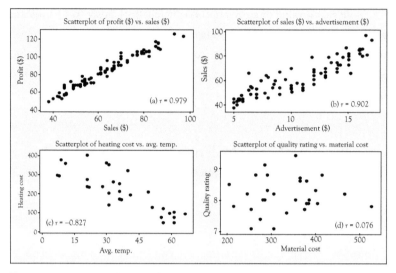

Figure 2.5 Scatterplots with correlation (r)

heating cost and the average temperature. Therefore, the coefficient of correlation (*r*) for this plot is negative (*r* = –0.827).

The correlation for the scatterplot in Figure 2.5(d) indicates a weak relationship between the quality rating and the material cost. This can also be seen from the coefficient of correlation that shows a low value of *r* = 0.076. These graphs are very helpful in describing bivariate relationships or the relationship between the two quantitative variables and can be easily created using computer packages such as MINITAB or Excel. Note that the plots in Figure 2.5(a) and (b) show strong positive correlation; (c) shows a negative correlation while (d) shows a weak correlation.

Summary

This chapter presented the mathematical model of simple linear regression. The simple linear regression method studies the linear relationship between two variables, the *dependent* or the *response variable* (*y*) and the *independent variable* or *predictor* (*x*).

Both the population and sample regression models were introduced. The model represented by $y = \beta_0 + \beta_1 x + \varepsilon$ can be viewed as a population regression model in which β_0 and β_1 are the parameters of the model. In the regression model, β_0 and β_1 are the unknown population parameters that must be estimated using the sample data. The estimates of β_0 and β_1 are denoted by b_0 and b_1 that provide the ***estimated regression equation*** given as $\hat{y} = b_0 + b_1x$. This regression equation is obtained using the ***least squares method***. The form of the regression equation is $y = b_0 + b_1x$, which is an equation of a straight line in the slope intercept form. We illustrated the least squares method using an example. The second part of the chapter examined the strength of the relationship between two quantitative variables: the covariance and the coefficient of correlation.

CHAPTER 3

Illustration of Least Squares Regression Method

In this chapter we provide a complete analysis of simple regression model. The least squares method that is the basis of regression model is used to estimate the best-fitting regression line. We will discuss the process of finding the regression equation, and calculate and interpret several measures to assess the quality of the regression model. The analysis in this chapter will help us understand and interpret the computer results in the subsequent chapters.

Analysis of a Simple Regression Problem

This section provides a complete analysis of a simple regression problem. The following example demonstrates the analysis steps and their interpretation for a regression problem involving two variables.

Problem Statement: Suppose an operations manager wants to predict the number of hours required or the time to produce a certain number of products. The past data for the number of units produced and the time in hours to produce those units are shown in the Table 3.1 (**Data File: Hours_Units**). This is a simple linear regression problem, so we have **one dependent** or **response variable** that we are trying to relate to **one independent variable** or **predictor**. Since we are trying to predict the number of hours using the number of units produced; **hours** is the **dependent** or **response** variable (y) and **number of units** is the **independent variable** or **predictor** (x).

For these data, we first calculate the intermediate values shown in Table 3.2. All these values are calculated using the observed values of x and y in Table 3.1. These intermediate values will be used in the computations related to simple regression analysis.

Table 3.1 Data for regression example

Obs. no.	1	2	3	4	5	6	7	8	9	10
Units (x)	932	951	531	766	814	914	899	535	554	445
Hours (y)	16.20	16.05	11.84	14.21	14.42	15.08	14.45	11.73	12.24	11.12

continued......

Obs. no.	11	12	13	14	15	16	17	18	19	20
Units (x)	704	897	949	632	477	754	819	869	1,035	646
Hours (y)	12.63	14.43	15.46	12.64	11.92	13.95	14.33	15.23	16.77	12.41

continued....

Obs. no.	21	22	23	24	25	26	27	28	29	30
Units (x)	1,055	875	969	1075	655	1,125	960	815	555	925
Hours (y)	17.00	15.50	16.20	17.50	12.92	18.20	15.10	14.00	12.20	15.50

Table 3.2 Intermediate calculations for data in Table 3.1

Number of observations, $n = 30$

$$\sum x = 24132$$
$$\sum y = 431.23$$
$$\sum xy = 357,055$$
$$\sum x^2 = 20,467,220$$
$$\sum y^2 = 6,302.3$$

$$\bar{x} = \frac{\sum x}{n} = 804.40$$
$$\bar{y} = \frac{\sum y}{n} = 14.374$$

We will demonstrate the use of computer packages such as MINITAB and Excel to analyze the simple regression problem but first we will explain the manual calculations and interpret the results. Readers will notice that all the formulas in the subsequent sections will be written in terms of the values calculated in Table 3.2.

Constructing a Scatterplot of the Data

We can use Excel or MINITAB to do a scatterplot of the data. From the data in Table 3.1, enter the units (x) in the first column and hours (y) in second column of Excel or MINITAB and construct a scatterplot.

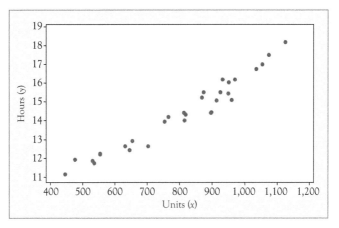

Figure 3.1 *Scatterplot of hours (y) and units (x)*

Figure 3.1 shows the scatterplot for this data. The data clearly show an increasing trend. It shows a linear relationship between x and y; therefore, the data can be approximated using a straight line with a positive slope.

Finding the Equation of the Best-Fitting Line (Estimated Line)

The equation of the estimated regression line is given by: $\hat{y} = b_0 + b_1 x$ where b_0 = y-intercept, and b_1 = slope. These are determined using the **least squares method**. Using the values in Table 3.2, first calculate the values of b_1 (the slope) and b_0 (the y-intercept) as follows.

$$b_1 = \frac{n\sum xy - \left(\sum x\right)\left(\sum y\right)}{n\sum x^2 - \left(\sum x\right)^2} = \frac{30(357055) - (24132)(431.23)}{30(20467220) - (24132)^2} = 0.00964$$

and

$$b_0 = \bar{y} - b_1\bar{x} = 14.374 - (0.00964)(804.40) = 6.62$$

Therefore, the equation of the estimated line,

$$\hat{y} = b_0 + b_1 x = 6.62 + 0.00964x$$

The regression equation or the equation of the "best" fitting line can also be written as:

$$Hours\ (y) = 6.62 + 0.00964\ Units\ (x)$$

or simply $\hat{y} = 6.62 + 0.00964x$

where y is the hours and x is the number of units produced. The hat (^) over y means that the line is estimated. Thus, the equation of the line, in fact, is an estimated equation of the best-fitting line. The line is also known as the **least squares line** which minimizes the sum of the squares of the errors. This means that when the line is placed over the scatterplot, the vertical distance from each of the points to the line is minimized. The vertical distance of each point from the estimated line is the error that is commonly known as the **residual**. Figure 3.2 shows the least squares line and the residuals. The residual for a point is given by $(y - \hat{y})$ that is the vertical distance of a point from the estimated line. We will provide more details on residuals later. Figure 3.3 shows the fitted regression line over the scatterplot.

Properties of the Least Squares Regression Line

The least squares regression line has the following important properties:

(i) The regression line passes through the point $(\bar{x}, \bar{y})$, the mean of x and y values. Therefore, to draw the regression line manually, we need to draw the line connecting the y-intercept b_0 value to the $(\bar{x}, \bar{y})$ point.

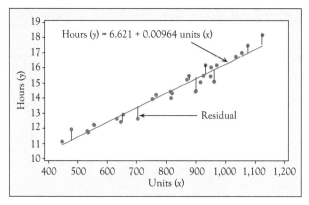

Figure 3.2 The least squares line and residuals

Note: The estimated line is denoted by $\hat{y}$ and the residual for a point y_i is given by $(y_i - \hat{y})$.

(ii) The sum of the deviations of the y values from the estimated regression line is zero, or

$$\sum (y - \hat{y}) = 0$$

This equation means that the positive and negative deviations from the estimated regression line cancel each other, so that the least squares regression line passes through the center of data points.

(iii) The sum of the square of the errors or residuals is a minimum and is denoted by SSE. Thus,

$$SSE = \sum (y - \hat{y})^2$$

(iv) The expected values of b_0 and b_1 are β_0 and β_1, or the least squares regression coefficients are unbiased estimates of β_0 and β_1.

Interpretation of the Fitted Regression Line

The estimated least squares line is of the form $y = b_0 + b_1 x$ where b_1 is the slope and b_0 is the y-intercept. The equation of the fitted line is

$$\hat{y} = 6.62 + 0.00964x$$

In this equation of the fitted line, 6.62 is the y-intercept and 0.00964 is the slope. This line provides the relationship between the hours and the number of units produced. The equation means that for each unit increase in x (the number of units produced), y (the number of hours) will increase by 0.00964. The value 6.62 represents the portion of the hours that is not affected by the number of units. Figure 3.3 shows the best-fitting line and its equation.

Making Predictions Using the Regression Line

The regression equation can be used to predict the number of hours required to produce a certain number of units. For example, suppose we

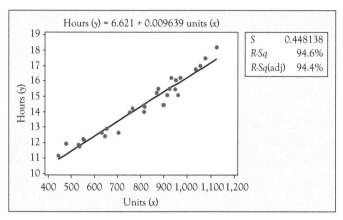

Figure 3.3 Fitted line regression plot

want to predict the number of hours (y) required to produce 900 units (x). This can be determined using the equation of the fitted line as:

Hours (y) = 6.62 + 0.00964 units (x)

Hours (y) = 6.62 + 0.00964 * (900) = 15.296 hours

Thus, it will take approximately 15.3 hours to produce 900 units of the product. Note that making a prediction outside of the range will introduce error in the predicted value. For example, if we want to predict the time for producing 2,000 units, this prediction will be outside the data range (see the data in Table 3.1, the range of x values is from 445 to 1,125). The value x = 2,000 is far greater than all the other x values in the data. From the scatterplot, a straight line fit with an increasing trend is evident for the data but we should be cautious about assuming that this straight line trend will continue to hold for values as large as x = 2,000. Therefore, it may not be reasonable to make this prediction for values that are far beyond or outside the range of the data values.

The Standard Error of the Estimate (s)

The standard error of the estimate measures the variation or scatter of the points around the fitted line of regression. This is measured in units of the response or dependent variable (y). The standard error of the estimate is analogous to the standard deviation. The standard deviation measures the variability around the mean, whereas the standard error of the estimate (s) measures the variability around the fitted line of regression. A large value of s indicates larger variation of the points around the fitted line of regression. The standard error of the estimate is calculated using the following formula:

$$s = \sqrt{\frac{\sum (y - \hat{y})^2}{n - 2}} \tag{3.1}$$

The equation can also be written as:

$$s = \sqrt{\frac{\sum y^2 - b_0 \sum y - b_1 \sum xy}{n - 2}} \tag{3.2}$$

Equation 3.1 measures the average deviation of the points from the fitted line of regression. Equation 3.2 is mathematically equivalent to Equation 3.1 and is computationally more efficient. Using the values of b_0, b_1, and the values in Table 3.2, the standard error of the estimate can be calculated as:

$$s = \sqrt{\frac{\sum y^2 - b_0 \sum y - b_1 \sum xy}{n - 2}}$$

$$= \sqrt{\frac{6302.3 - 6.62(431.23) - 0.00964(357055)}{28}} = 0.4481$$

Thus,

$$s = 0.4481$$

A small value of s indicates less scatter of the data points around the fitted line of regression (see Figure 3.3). The value s = 0.4481 indicates that the average deviation is 0.4481 hours (measured in units of dependent variable y). Note: These values were verified using MINITAB.

The Coefficient of Determination (r²) and Its Meaning

The coefficient of determination r^2 is an indication of how well the independent variable predicts the dependent variable. In other words, it is used to judge the adequacy of the regression model. The value of r^2 lies between 0 and 1 ($0 \leq r^2 \leq 1$) or 0% to 100%. The closer the value of r^2 to 1 or 100%, the better is the model because the r^2 value indicates the amount of variation in the data explained by the regression model. Figure 3.4 shows the relationship between the explained, unexplained, and the total variation.

In regression, the total sum of squares is partitioned into two components, the regression sum of squares and the error sum of squares giving the following relationship:

$$SST = SSR + SSE \tag{3.3}$$

SST = total sum of squares for y

SSR = regression sum of squares (measures the variability in y, accounted for by the regression line, also known as explained variation)

SSE = error sum of squares (measures the variation due to the error or residual). This is also known as unexplained variation).

y_i = any point i; $\bar{y}$ = average of the y values

From Figure 3.4, the SST and SSE are calculated as

$$SST = \sum (y - \bar{y})^2 = \sum y^2 - \frac{\left(\sum y\right)^2}{n} \tag{3.4}$$

and

$$SSE = \sum (y - \hat{y})^2 = \sum y^2 - b_0 \sum y - b_1 \sum xy \tag{3.5}$$

Note that we can calculate SSR by calculating SST and SSE since,

$$SST = SSR + SSE \text{ or } SSR = SST - SSE$$

Using the SSR and SST values, the coefficient of determination r^2 is calculated using

$$r^2 = \frac{SSR}{SST} \tag{3.6}$$

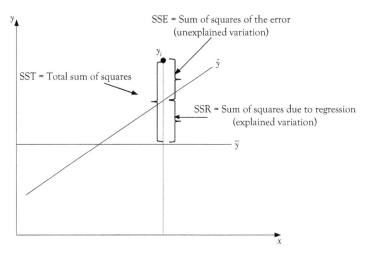

Figure 3.4 SST = SSR + SSE

The coefficient of determination r^2 is used to measure the goodness of fit for the regression equation. It measures the variation in y explained by the variation in independent variable x. The r^2 can be seen as the ratio of the explained variation to the total variation.

The calculation of r^2 is explained as follows. First, calculate SST and SSE using Equations 3.4 and 3.5 and the values in Table 3.2.

$$\text{SST} = \sum (y - \bar{y})^2 = \sum y^2 - \frac{\left(\sum y\right)^2}{n} = 6302.3 - \frac{(431.23)^2}{30} = 103.680$$

$$\text{SSE} = \sum (y - \hat{y})^2 = \sum y^2 - b_0 \sum y - b_1 \sum xy$$

$$= 6302.3 - 6.62(431.23) - 0.00964(357055) = 5.623$$

Since

$$\text{SST} = \text{SSR} + \text{SSE}$$

Therefore,   SSR = SST − SSE = 103.680 − 5.623 = 98.057   (3.7)

and

$$r^2 = \frac{\text{SSR}}{\text{SST}} = \frac{98.057}{103.680} = 0.946$$

or, $r^2 = 94.6\%$

This means that 94.6% variation in the dependent variable y is explained by the variation in x and 5.4% of the variation is due to unexplained reasons or error.

The Coefficient of Correlation (r) and Its Meaning

The coefficient of correlation, r can be calculated by taking the square root of r^2 or,

$$r = \sqrt{r^2}$$ (3.8)

Therefore,

$$r = \sqrt{r^2} = \sqrt{0.946} = 0.973$$

In this case, $r = 97.3\%$ indicates a strong positive correlation between x and y. Note that r is positive if the slope b_1 is positive indicating a positive correlation between x and y. The value of r is between -1 and $+1$.

$$-1 \le r \le 1$$ (3.9)

The value of r determines the correlation between x and y variables. The closer the value of r to -1 or $+1$, the stronger is the correlation between x and y.

The value of the coefficient of correlation r can be positive or negative. The value of r is positive if the slope b_1 is positive; it is negative if b_1 is negative. If r is positive it indicates a positive correlation, whereas a negative r indicates a negative correlation. The coefficient of correlation r can also be calculated using the following formula:

$$r = \frac{\sum xy - \dfrac{\left(\sum x\right)\left(\sum y\right)}{n}}{\sqrt{\sum x^2 - \dfrac{\left(\sum x\right)^2}{n}} * \sqrt{\sum y^2 - \dfrac{\left(\sum y\right)^2}{n}}}$$ (3.10)

Using the values in Table 3.2, we can calculate r from Equation 3.10.

Confidence Interval for the Mean (Average) Response y for a Given Value of x

A confidence interval may be constructed for the mean or average value of y for a given or specified value of x, say x_0. This is a confidence interval denoted by $\mu_{y|x_0}$.

Note that $\hat{y}$ is the point estimate of y and will be used to build the confidence interval around the mean response. The accuracy of this confidence interval depends on the number of observations n, the variability in the sample, and the value of $x = x_0$.

A $(1 - \alpha)$ 100% confidence interval around the true regression line at $x = x_0$ may be calculated using the following expression:

$$\hat{y} \pm t_{\alpha/2, n-2}(s) \sqrt{\frac{1}{n} + \frac{(x_0 - \bar{x})^2}{\sum x^2 - \frac{\left(\sum x\right)^2}{n}}} \qquad (3.11)$$

Equation 3.11 can be written in expanded form as follows:

$$\hat{y} - t_{\alpha/2, n-2}(s) \sqrt{\frac{1}{n} + \frac{(x_0 - \bar{x})^2}{\sum x^2 - \frac{\left(\sum x\right)^2}{n}}} \leq \mu_{y|x_0}$$

$$\leq \hat{y} + t_{\alpha/2, n-2}(s) \sqrt{\frac{1}{n} + \frac{(x_0 - \bar{x})^2}{\sum x^2 - \frac{\left(\sum x\right)^2}{n}}} \qquad (3.12)$$

where $\hat{y}$ is the point estimate of y for a given x:

$t_{n-2, \alpha/2}$ is the t-value for $(n - 2)$ degrees of freedom and $\alpha/2$,

S is the standard error of the estimate, and

$$s \sqrt{\frac{1}{n} + \frac{(x_0 - \bar{x})^2}{\sum x^2 - \frac{\left(\sum x\right)^2}{n}}} = S_y; \text{ the standard deviation of } y$$

Calculation of Confidence Interval

Suppose we want to calculate a 95% confidence interval for the average value of hours (y) for $x = 951$ units. This can be calculated as follows.

The regression equation for our example problem is

$$\hat{y} = 6.62 + 0.00964x$$

Therefore, $\hat{y}$ for $x = 951$

$$\hat{y} = 6.62 + 0.00964(951) = 15.79$$

Now we can use Equation 3.11 to calculate the confidence interval. In this equation, $t_{\alpha/2,n-2} = t_{0.025,28} = 2.0484$ (from the t-table),

S = standard error of estimate = 0.4481 (calculated earlier using Equation 3.2) and

$$\sqrt{\frac{1}{n} + \frac{(x_0 - \bar{x})^2}{\sum x^2 - \frac{(\sum x)^2}{n}}} = \sqrt{\frac{1}{30} + \frac{(951 - 804.40)^2}{20467220 - \frac{(24132)^2}{30}}} = 0.232$$

Substituting the values in the confidence interval Equation 3.11

$$\hat{y} \pm t_{\alpha/2,n-2} s \sqrt{\frac{1}{n} + \frac{(x_0 - \bar{x})^2}{\sum x^2 - \frac{(\sum x)^2}{n}}} = 15.79 \pm 2.0484(0.4481)(0.232)$$

which gives a confidence interval of 15.6 to 16.0 hours. The confidence interval is written as:

$$15.6 \le \mu_{y|x_0} \le 16.0$$

This is the confidence interval estimate for the average hours required for all production units of 951. The confidence interval means that we are 95% confident that on the average 15.6 to 16.0 hours will be required to produce 951 units.

Prediction Interval for an Individual Response, $\hat{y}$

The regression equation is also used to predict or forecast a new or future value of the dependent value y for a given or specified value of x, the

independent value. This is one of the important and common applications of the regression model. The individual predicted value of y is
denoted by y_{x_0} for $x = x_0$.

In general, a $(1 - \alpha)$ 100% prediction interval is calculated for y_{x_0}.
The interval is not referred to as a confidence interval because y_{x_0} is a
random variable and not a parameter. The $(1 - \alpha)$ 100% prediction
interval for a future predicted value is given by:

$$\hat{y} \pm t_{\alpha/2, n-2}(s) \sqrt{1 + \frac{1}{n} + \frac{(x_0 - \bar{x})^2}{\sum x^2 - \frac{\left(\sum x\right)^2}{n}}} \qquad (3.13)$$

Equation 3.13 is very similar to the confidence interval formula
of Equations 3.11 or 3.12 except that a "1" is added to the expression
under the square root. It makes the prediction interval wider than the
confidence interval. While the confidence interval provides the average
response for a given value of x, the prediction interval predicts the interval
for an individual response for a given value of x. This is the reason that the
prediction interval is wider than the confidence interval.

Calculation for Prediction Interval

Suppose we want to calculate a 95% prediction interval for an individual
value of hours (y) for $x = 951$ units. This can be calculated as follows. Note
that the regression equation for our example problem is

$$\hat{y} = 6.62 + 0.00964x$$

and the $\hat{y}$ for $x = 951$ can be calculated as follows:

$$\hat{y} = 6.62 + 0.00964(951) = 15.79 \text{ hours}$$

Now we can use Equation 3.13 to calculate the prediction interval as
follows:

$$t_{\alpha/2, n-2} = t_{0.025, 28} = 2.0484 \quad \text{(from the } t\text{-table)}$$

S = standard error of estimate = 0.4481 (calculated earlier using Equation 3.2)

and

$$\sqrt{1+\frac{1}{n}+\frac{(x_0-\bar{x})^2}{\sum x^2-\frac{(\sum x)^2}{n}}} = \sqrt{1+\frac{1}{30}+\frac{(951-804.40)^2}{20467220-\frac{(24132)^2}{30}}} = 1.0265$$

Substituting the values in the prediction interval Equation 3.13

$$\hat{y}\pm t_{\alpha/2,n-2}s\sqrt{1+\frac{1}{n}+\frac{(x_0-\bar{x})^2}{\sum x^2-\frac{(\sum x)^2}{n}}} = 15.79\pm 2.0484(0.4481)(1.0265)$$

This provides an interval of 14.85 to 16.73 hours. The prediction interval is written as:

$$14.85 \le \mu_{y_{x_0}} \le 16.73$$

This is the prediction interval estimate for an individual response (hours) for a given value of x.

Testing the Significance of Regression

The following three tests can be conducted to test the significance of regression:

1. Test for the significance using the coefficient of the regression slope or t-test
2. Test for the significance of regression using the F-test
3. Test for the significance using the correlation coefficient (r)

In the following, we have demonstrated the tests for significance of regression for our example problem (Table 3.1 data).

Test 1: Testing the Regression Slope—t-test

From our earlier discussion, we know that the regression model is given by $y = \beta_0 + \beta_1 x + \varepsilon$ where β_1 is the population slope. Test for the significance of regression involves testing whether there is a linear relationship between x and y. If there is a linear relationship between x and y, we must have $\beta_1 \neq 0$. This can be tested by performing a hypothesis test about β_1 using the sample data. The steps for conducting this test are discussed as follows.

Step 1: State the null and alternate hypotheses

$$H_0 : \beta_1 = 0$$
$$H_1 : \beta_1 \neq 0$$

(3.14)

The null hypothesis states that there is no relationship between x and y, or the slope is zero. The alternate hypothesis states that there is an evidence of a linear relationship between x and y. If the null hypothesis H_0 is rejected, we can conclude that there is a significant relationship between the two variables.

Step 2: Specify the test statistic to test the hypothesis

The test statistic uses the sample slope b_1, which is the unbiased estimator of β_1. The sampling distribution b_1 follows a normal distribution with the following expected value and standard deviation: $E(b_1) = \beta_1$ and

$$\sigma_{b_1} = \frac{\sigma}{\sqrt{\sum x^2 - \frac{\left(\sum x\right)^2}{N}}}$$

Since, σ and σ_{b_1} are unknown, we estimate σ by s and σ_{b_1} the standard deviation of b_1 using

$$s_{b_1} = \frac{s}{\sqrt{\sum x^2 - \frac{\left(\sum x\right)^2}{n}}}$$

Using these sample estimates, the test statistic is given by:

$$t_{n-2} = \frac{b_1}{s_{b_1}}$$

(3.15)

In Equation 3.15, b_1 is the slope and s_{b_1} is the standard deviation of the slope b_1.

Step 3: Calculate the value of the test statistic

The calculations are shown as follows. We know that the slope b_1 = 0.00964. The value S = 0.4481 is the standard error of the estimate (calculated earlier). Therefore:

$$s_{b_1} = \frac{s}{\sqrt{\sum x^2 - \frac{\left(\sum x\right)^2}{n}}} = \frac{0.4481}{\sqrt{20467220 - \frac{(24132)^2}{30}}} = 0.000436$$

which gives the test-statistic value of

$$t_{n-2} = \frac{b_1}{s_{b_1}} = \frac{0.00964}{0.000436} = 22.11$$

Step 4: Specify the critical value

The critical values for a 5% level of significance are:

$$t_{n-2, \alpha/2} = t_{28, 0.025} = 2.048 \text{ (from the } t\text{-table)}$$

The critical values are shown in Figure 3.5.

Step 5: Specify the decision rule

Reject H_0 if the test statistic value t_{n-2} > 2.048

or,   if t_{n-2} < −2.048

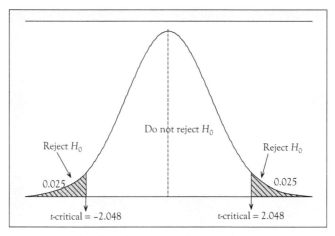

Figure 3.5 Critical values for testing the significance of regression

Step 6: Reach a decision and state your conclusion

The test statistic value is $t_{n-2} = 22.11 > 2.048$; therefore, reject H_0 and conclude that the regression is significant overall.

Test 2: Testing for the Significance of Regression Using the F-test

In the simple regression, the F-test will provide the same conclusion as the t-test. The F-test is based on the F-distribution. Recall that this distribution compares the ratio of two variances. The test for the significance of regression is based on the development of two independent estimates of the variances: the mean square due to regression (MSR) and the mean square due to error (MSE). MSR and MSE are given by:

$$\text{MSR} = \frac{\text{SSR}}{\text{Regression degrees of freedom}} \text{ and}$$

$$\text{MSE} = \frac{\text{SSE}}{\text{Error or residual degrees of freedom}}$$

The regression degrees of freedom is given by k and the error degrees of freedom is given by $(n-2)$ where k is the number of independent variables and n is the number of observations. For simple linear regression, the regression degree of freedom is always equal to one.

If the null hypothesis ($H_0 : \beta_1 = 0$) is true, the ratio of two variances MSR/MSE follows an F-distribution with numerator degrees of freedom equal to 1 and the denominator degrees of freedom equal to $n - 2$. When $\beta_1 = 0$, the ratio MSR/MSE is 1 or close to 1. On the other hand, if $\beta_1 \neq 0$, the MSR value will be much larger than the MSE. The larger values of the ratio MSR/MSE will lead to the rejection of the null hypothesis indicating a significant relationship between x and y. The steps for conducting the F-test are described as follows.

Step 1: State the null and alternate hypotheses

$$H_0 : \beta_1 = 0$$
$$H_1 : \beta_1 \neq 0$$

Step 2: Specify the test statistic to test the hypothesis

$$F = \frac{\text{MSR}}{\text{MSE}} \qquad (3.16)$$

Step 3: Calculate the value of the test statistic
Note that MSR = SSR/k and MSE = SSE/$n - 2$ where k is the regression degrees of freedom, which is equal to the number of independent variables. The value of k is always equal to 1 for simple regression. For our example, $n = 30$ therefore, the error degrees of freedom are 28. We have already calculated the values of SSR and SSE using Equation 3.7. These values are SSE = 5.623 and SSR = 98.057. Using these values,

$$F = \frac{\text{MSR}}{\text{MSE}} = \frac{\text{SSR} / k}{\text{SSE} / n - 2} = \frac{98.057 / 1}{5.623 / 28} = 488.28$$

Step 4: Specify the critical value
The critical value:

$$F_{k, n-2, \alpha} = F_{1, 28, 0.05} = 4.196 \text{ (from the } F\text{-table)}$$

Step 5: Specify the decision rule

$$\text{Reject } H_0 \text{ if the test statistic value } F > F_{critical}$$

Step 6: Reach a decision and state your conclusion
The test statistic value $F = 488.28$ is greater than the critical value of F (4.196); therefore, reject H_0 and conclude that the regression is significant overall.

Test 3: Test for the Significance Using the Correlation Coefficient (r)

The test for the significance for a linear relationship between x and y can also be performed using the sample correlation coefficient r. This test conducts a hypothesis test to determine whether the population correlation is equal to zero. The steps for conducting this test are described as follows.

Step 1: State the null and alternate hypotheses

$$H_0 : \rho = 0$$
$$H_1 : \rho \neq 0$$

(3.17)

where ρ (read as "rho") denotes the population correlation coefficient. The null hypothesis indicates no correlation between x and y, whereas the alternate hypothesis indicates an evidence of correlation. If the null hypothesis is rejected, we conclude that there is evidence of a linear relationship between x and y and the regression is significant.

Step 2: Specify the test statistic to test the hypothesis and calculate the test statistic value
The test statistic and its value for this test are given by:

$$t_{n-2} = \frac{r}{\sqrt{\dfrac{1-r^2}{n-2}}} = \frac{0.973}{\sqrt{\dfrac{1-(0.973)^2}{28}}} = 22.31$$

Note that r is the sample coefficient of correlation that can be calculated using Equation 3.10 or can be determined by taking the square root of coefficient of determination r^2.

Step 3: Specify the critical value

The *critical values* to test the hypothesis are given by

$$\pm t_{n-2,\,\alpha/2} = \pm t_{28,0.025} = \pm 2.048 \text{ (from the } t\text{-table)}$$

(where the number of observations, $n = 30$ and $\alpha = 0.05$).
The critical values are shown in Figure 3.5.

Step 4: Specify the decision rule

Reject H_0 if the test statistic value $t_{n-2} > 2.048$ or if $t_{n-2} < -2.048$

Step 5: Reach a decision and state your conclusion

Since $t_{n-2} = 22.31$ is greater than the critical value 2.048, we reject the null hypothesis in Equation 3.17 and conclude that there is an evidence of linear relationship between x and y.

Summary

This chapter illustrated the least squares method that is the basis of regression model. The process of finding the regression equation using the least squares method was demonstrated. The analysis of this simple regression problem was presented by calculating and interpreting several measures. As a part of the analysis, the following analyses were performed: (a) constructing a scatterplot of the data, (b) finding the equation of the best-fitting line, (c) interpreting the fitted regression line, and (d) making predictions using the fitted regression equation. Other important measures critical to assessing the quality of the regression model were calculated and explained. These measures include: (a) the standard error of the estimate (s) that measures the variation or scatter of the points around the fitted line of regression, (b) the coefficient of determination (r^2) that measures how well the independent variable predicts the dependent variable or the percent of variation in the dependent variable y explained by the variation in the independent variable x, and (c) the coefficient of correlation (r) that measures the strength of relationship between x and y. We also calculated and interpreted: (a) the confidence interval for the mean (average) response y for a given value of x and (b) the prediction interval for an individual response. Finally, the tests for the significance of regression—the t-test and F-test were conducted. The steps for these tests were outlined.

CHAPTER 4

Regression Analysis Using a Computer

This chapter provides a detailed stepwise computerized analysis of regression models. In real world, software is almost always used to analyze regression problems. A number of software are currently available for analysis of regression models, of which MINITAB, Excel, SAS, SPSS are a few to name.

In this text, we have used Excel and MINITAB® software to analyze the regression models. The applications of simple, multiple, and higher order regressions using Excel and MINITAB are demonstrated in this and the subsequent chapters. The reason for using Excel is that it is the most widely used spreadsheet program in both industry and academia. MINITAB is a leading software for statistics, data analysis, and quality improvement and is used by 90% of Fortune 100 companies. It is also widely used as a teaching tool in colleges and universities. Note that Excel is a spreadsheet program and was not designed for performing in-depth statistical analysis. It can be used for analyses up to a certain level but lacks the capability of producing in-depth reports for higher order regression models. If one performs regression analysis using a substantial amount of data and needs more detailed analyses, the use of statistical packages such as MINITAB, SAS®, and SPSS® are recommended.

Besides these, a number of software, including R, Stata, and others, are readily available and widely used in research and data analysis. We have provided a detailed description of regression analysis using Excel and MINITAB. The steps to create data file and the analysis procedures are outlined in the following table.

Simple Regression Using Excel

The instructions to run the simple regression using Excel are in *Appendix A_Table A.1*, and also listed in Table 4.1. *The Excel and MINITAB data files can be downloaded from the website.*

The partial regression output will be displayed. If one checks the boxes under **Residuals** and the **Line Fit Plots**, the residuals and fitted line plot will be displayed. In the later section, we will describe the computer results using MINITAB, including the residuals and residual plots.

Table 4.2 shows the output with regression statistics. We calculated all these manually except the adjusted *R-Square* in the previous chapter. The regression equation can be read from the ***Coefficients*** column. The regression coefficients are b_0 and b_1: the *y*-intercept and the slope. In the

Table 4.1 Excel instructions for regression

1. Label columns A and B of Excel worksheet with Units (x) and Hours (y) and enter the data of Table 3.1 (Chapter 3) or, open the Excel data file: **Hours_Units.xlsx** (Table A.1, Appendix A)
2. Click the Data tab on the main menu
3. Click Data Analysis tab (on far right)
4. Select Regression
5. Select Hours (x) for Input y range and Units (x) for Input x range (including the labels)
6. Check the Labels box
7. Click on the circle to the left of Output Range, click on the box next to output range and specify where you want to store the output by clicking a blank cell (or select New Worksheet Ply)
8. Check the Line Fit Plot under residuals. Click OK
   You may check the boxes under residuals and normal probability plot as desired.

Table 4.2 Excel regression output

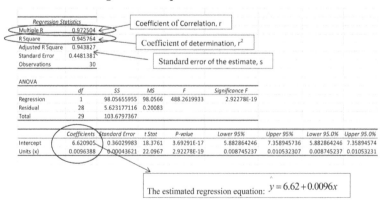

Regression Statistics	
Multiple R	0.972504
R Square	0.945764
Adjusted R Square	0.943827
Standard Error	0.448138
Observations	30

Coefficient of Correlation, r
Coefficient of determination, r^2
Standard error of the estimate, s

ANOVA

	df	SS	MS	F	Significance F
Regression	1	98.05655955	98.0566	488.2619933	2.92278E-19
Residual	28	5.623177116	0.20083		
Total	29	103.6797367			

	Coefficients	Standard Error	t Stat	P-value	Lower 95%	Upper 95%	Lower 95.0%	Upper 95.0%
Intercept	6.620905	0.36029983	18.3761	3.69291E-17	5.882864246	7.358945736	5.882864246	7.35894574
Units (x)	0.0096388	0.00043621	22.0967	2.92278E-19	0.008745237	0.010532307	0.008745237	0.01053231

The estimated regression equation: $\hat{y} = 6.62 + 0.0096x$

coefficients column, 6.620904991 is the *y*-intercept and 0.009638772 is the slope. The regression equation from this table is:

$$\hat{y} = 6.62 + 0.00964x$$

This is the same equation we obtained earlier using manual calculations in Chapter 3.

The Coefficient of Determination (r²) using Excel

The values of SST and SSR were calculated manually in the previous chapter. Recall that in regression, the total sum of squares is partitioned into two components; the regression sum of squares (SSR) and the error sum of squares (SSE), giving the following relationship: SST = SSR + SSE. The coefficient of determination r^2, which is also the measure of goodness of fit for the regression equation, can be calculated using

$$r^2 = \frac{SSR}{SST}$$

The values of SSR, SSE, and SST can be obtained using the analysis of variance (ANOVA) table of regression output, which is part of the regression analysis output of Excel. Table 4.3 shows the Excel regression output with SSR and SST values. Using these values, the coefficient of determination, $r^2 = $ SSR / SST = 0.9458. This value is reported under regression statistics in Table 4.3.

The *t*-test and *F*-test for the significance of regression can be easily performed using the information in the Excel computer output. Table 4.4

Table 4.3 Excel regression output (1)

Regression Statistics	
Multiple R	0.972504
R Square	0.945764
Adjusted R Square	0.943827
Standard Error	0.4481381
Observations	30

SSR=98.056556   SST=103.67974

SSE=5.623177

ANOVA

	df	SS	MS	F	Significance F
Regression	1	98.05655955	98.0866	488.2619953	2.92278E-19
Residual	28	5.623177116	0.20083		
Total	29	103.6797367			

	Coefficients	Standard Error	t Stat	P-value	Lower 95%	Upper 95%	Lower 95.0%	Upper 95.0%
Intercept	6.620905	0.36029983	18.3761	3.69291E-17	5.882864246	7.358945736	5.882864246	7.35894574
Units (x)	0.0096388	0.00043621	22.0967	2.92278E-19	0.008745237	0.010532307	0.008745237	0.01053231

Table 4.4 *Excel regression output (2)*

Regression Statistics	
Multiple R	0.972504
R Square	0.945764
Adjusted R Square	0.943827
Standard Error	0.4481381
Observations	30

$r = 0.9725$

$MSR = 98.0566$

$$F = \frac{MSR}{MSE} = 488.2619$$

ANOVA

	df	SS	MS	F	Significance F
Regression	1	98.05655955	98.0566	488.2619933	2.92278E-19
Residual	28	5.623177116	0.20083		
Total	29	103.6797367			

$MSE = 0.20083$

	Coefficients	Standard Error	t Stat	P-value	Lower 95%	Upper 95%	Lower 95.0%	Upper 95.0%
Intercept	6.620905	0.36029983	18.3761	3.69291E-17	5.882864246	7.358945736	5.882864246	7.35894574
Units (x)	0.0096388	0.00043621	22.0967	2.92278E-19	0.008745237	0.010532307	0.008745237	0.01053231

b_1 s_{b_1} t_{n-2} *p-value*

shows the Excel regression output with the ANOVA table. (The table shows other computed values that will be used for analysis.)

(1)   Conducting the *t*-test using the regression output in Table 4.4
The test statistic for conducting the significance of regression is given by the following equation:

$$t_{n-2} = \frac{b_1}{s_{b_1}}$$

The values of b_1, s_{b_1} and the test-statistic value t_{n-2} are labeled in Table 4.4.

Using the test-statistic value, the hypothesis test for the significance of regression can be conducted. This test has been explained in the previous chapter. The appropriate hypotheses for the test are:

$$H_0 : \beta_1 = 0$$
$$H_1 : \beta_1 \neq 0$$

The null hypothesis states that the slope of the regression line is zero. Thus, if the regression is significant, the null hypothesis must be rejected. A convenient way of testing the preceding hypotheses is to use the *p*-value approach. The test statistic value t_{n-2} and the corresponding p values are reported in the regression output table. Note that the p is very close to zero ($p = 2.92278E-19$). If we test the hypothesis at a 5% level of significance ($\alpha = 0.05$) then $p = 0.000$ is less than $\alpha = 0.05$; we reject the null hypothesis and conclude that the regression is significant overall.

(2)   Conducting the *F*-test using the regression output in Table 4.4.
The ANOVA table of the regression output in Table 4.4 provides the values for MSR, MSE, and the test-statistic value. It also provided the significance *F* or the *p*-value for conducting the test. Using the test-statistic value and the *p*-value approach, the decision rule for the test can be given by:

$$\text{If } p \geq \alpha; \text{ do not reject } H_0$$

$$\text{If } p < \alpha; \text{ reject } H_0$$

Suppose we want to conduct the test at 5% level of significance, or at $\alpha = 0.05$. Since $p = 0.000$ is less than $\alpha = 0.05$; we reject H_0 and conclude that the regression is significant. This test is described in more detail in the computer analysis part.

Simple Regression Using MINITAB

We have provided a detailed regression analysis using MINITAB. The steps to create the data file and run the regression are explained as follows.

Step 1: Label columns C1 and C2 of MINITAB worksheet with Units (*x*) and Hours (*y*) and enter the data of Table 3.1 (from Chapter 3) or open the data file **Hours_Units**. Column C1 contains the independent variable or predictor (units, *x*) and column C2 contains the response variable (hours, *y*).

Step 2: Construct a scatter plot of the data. Follow the instructions in *Appendix A_Table A.2*. The scatterplot will be similar to Figure 4.1 without the line through the points.

Note: Readers can download a free 30 days trial copy of the MINITAB version 17 software from www.minitab.com

The scatter plot clearly shows an increasing or direct relationship between the number of units produced (*x*) and the number of hours (*y*). Therefore, the data may be approximated by a straight line of the form $y = b_0 + b_1 x$, where b_0 is the *y*-intercept and b_1 is the slope.

Step 3: Run the regression model with fitted line plot option. **The instructions are in *Appendix A _Table A.3*.**

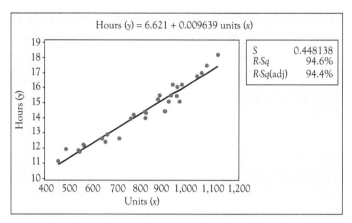

Figure 4.1 Fitted line and regression equation

Table 4.5 The regression analysis and analysis of variance tables using MINITAB

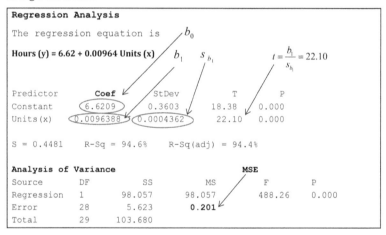

The fitted line plot with the regression equation from MINITAB is shown in Figure 4.1. Also, the "**Regression Analysis**" and "**Analysis of Variance**" tables shown in Table 4.5 will be displayed. We will first analyze the regression and the analysis of variance tables and then provide further analysis.

Analysis of Regression Output in Table 4.5

Refer to the **Regression Analysis** part. In this table, the regression equation is printed as **Hours (y) = 6.62 + 0.00964 Units (x)**. This is the equation of the best-fitting line using the least squares method. Just below the regression equation, a table is printed that describes the model in more detail. The values under the **Coef** column means coefficients. The values in this column refer to the regression coefficients b_0 and b_1, where b_0 is the y-intercept or constant and b_1 is the slope of the regression line. Under the **Predictor**, the value of Units (x) is 0.0096388, which is b_1 (or the slope of the fitted line). The **Constant** is 6.6209. These values form the regression equation.

The **StDev** in the printout means standard deviation and contains the standard deviation of the constant b_0 and the slope b_1. The standard deviation of the slope is referred to as s_{b_1} and is an important quantity. In the regression analysis printout, $s_{b_1} = 0.0004362$. We will discuss this later.

The **T** column contains the values that can be used for conducting t-tests for the slope and the y-intercept or the constant. The t-test for the slope is conducted to determine the significance of the regression or to determine whether there is an evidence of a linear relationship between the dependent and independent variable. In the **T** column, the T value for the constant is 18.38, which is obtained by dividing the constant ($b_0 = 6.6209$) by the standard deviation of b_0, which is 0.3603. Thus, $6.6209/0.3603 = 18.38$ is the T value for the constant. This value is not of much importance since we do not conduct a t-test for the constant. The **T** value for the slope is an important quantity, which is used in conducting the t-test for the slope to determine the significance of regression. The T value for the slope is 22.10 in the printout. This value is obtained by:

$$t = \frac{b_1}{s_{b_1}} = \frac{0.0096388}{0.0004362} = 22.10$$

Finally, the **p-column** contains the associated probabilities with the T values. The probability p of the given T value can be used to test the hypothesis using the p-value approach. Later in our analysis, we will explain the hypothesis test and the use of p-value.

Further Analysis of Regression Output in Table 4.5

Refer to Table 4.5:

1. The regression equation or the equation of the "best" fitting line is:

$$\text{Hours } (y) = 6.62 + 0.00964 \text{ Units } (x)$$

or

$$\hat{y} = 6.62 + 0.00964x$$

where y is the Hours and x is the units produced.

This line minimizes the sum of the squares of the errors. This means that when the line is placed over the scatter plot, the vertical distance from each of the points to the line is minimum. The **error** or the **residual** is the vertical distance of each point from the estimated line.

The estimated least squares line is of the form $y = b_0 + b_1 x$, where b_1 is the slope and b_0 is the y-intercept. In the regression equation: Hours $(y) = 6.62 + 0.00964$ Units (x), where 6.62 is the y-intercept and 0.00964 is the slope. This line provides the relationship between the hours and the number of units produced. The equation states that for each unit increase in x (the number of units produced), the value of dependent variable, y (the number of hours) will increase by 0.00964.

2. The Standard Error of the Estimate(s)

The standard error of the estimate measures the variation of the points around the fitted line of regression. This is measured in units of the response or dependent variable (y).

In regression analysis, the standard error of the estimate is reported as s. The value of s is reported in Table 4.5 under "**Regression Analysis.**" This value is:

$$s = 0.4481$$

A small value of s indicates less scatter of the points around the fitted line of regression.

3. The Coefficient of Determination (r^2)

The coefficient of determination, r^2, is an indicator of how well the independent variable predicts the dependent variable. In other words, it is used to judge the adequacy of the regression model. The value of r^2 lies between 0 and 1 ($0 \le r^2 \le 1$) or 0% to 100%. The closer the value of r^2 to 1 or 100%, the better is the model. The r^2 value indicates the amount of variability in the data explained by the regression model.

In our example, the r^2 value is 94.6% (Table 4.5, regression analysis). The value of r^2 is reported as:

$$R\text{-}Sq = 94.6\%$$

This means that 94.6% variation in the dependent variable y can be explained by the variation in x and 5.4% of the variation is due to unexplained reasons or error.

The $R\text{-}Sq(\text{adj}) = 94.4\%$ next to the value of r^2 in the regression output is the r^2-adjusted value. This is the r^2 value adjusted for the degrees of freedom. This value has more importance in multiple regression.

> **Analysis of variance (ANOVA) table: Interpretation and testing hypothesis using this table**

The analysis of variance table is printed just below the regression analysis (see Table 4.5). This table is used to test the significance of the regression model discussed earlier.

As discussed earlier, the ANOVA table can be used to test the evidence of a linear relationship between x and y, the independent and dependent variable, respectively. The hypotheses $H_0 : \beta_1 = 0$ versus $H_1 : \beta_1 \neq 0$ is tested for this purpose. If the null hypothesis is *not* rejected, we conclude that there is no linear relationship between x and y.

Confidence Interval for the Slope β_1

In the estimated equation of the regression line:

$$\hat{y} = b_0 + b_1 x$$

b_1 and b_0 are the point estimates of the slope and the y-intercept.

For our example, the equation of the estimated line is $\hat{y} = 6.62 + 0.00964x$, where $b_0 = 6.62$ and $b_1 = 0.00964$. In many cases, we might be interested in the confidence interval of the slope. The width of this confidence interval is a measure of the quality of the regression line. In other words, the narrower the width of this confidence interval, the more reliable is our estimate of the population slope β_1. As a result, the model will be more accurate and the independent variable x will be a more reliable predictor of the dependent variable y.

The $(1 - \alpha)$ 100% confidence interval for the population slope β_1 is calculated using the following expression:

$$b_1 - t_{n-2,\alpha/2}s_{b_1} \leq \beta_1 \leq b_1 + t_{n-2,\alpha/2}s_{b_1} \tag{4.1}$$

where $t_{n-2,\alpha/2}$ is the t-value for $(n - 2)$ degrees of freedom and $\alpha/2$, where n is the number of observations, b_1 is the point estimate of the slope (slope from the fitted regression line), and s_{b_1} is the standard deviation of this slope.

A 95% confidence interval for the population slope β_1 is shown as follows. Note that for our example, $b_1 = 0.00964$, $t_{n-2,\alpha/2} = t_{28,0.025} = 2.0484$ and $s_{b_1} = 0.0004362$. In the computer printout, Table 4.5 above, these values are labeled except for the $t_{n-2,\alpha/2} = t_{28,0.025} = 2.0484$, which is the value from the t-table. Substituting these values in the confidence interval formula (Equation 4.1):

$$0.00964 - (2.0484)(0.0004362) \leq \beta_1 \leq 0.00964 + (2.0484)(0.0004362)$$
$$0.00964 - 0.000894 \leq \beta_1 \leq 0.00964 + 0.000894$$
$$0.0087 \leq \beta_1 \leq 0.01053$$

This confidence interval means that we are 95% confident that the value of the estimated slope $b_1 = 0.00964$ is within 0.000894 of the actual slope β_1. This width is very small, indicating that the regression line is a reliable predictor of the dependent variable.

Confidence and Prediction Intervals in Simple Linear Regression Using MINITAB

The confidence and prediction intervals can be calculated using commands in MINITAB. The instructions for computing confidence and prediction intervals are in *Appendix A_Table A.4*. Following the instructions, we can calculate fits, standard deviation of fits, 95% confidence and prediction intervals and store them in separate columns. Note that these columns are stored as PFITS (for predicted fitted values), PSEFITS (standard deviation of the fits), CLIM and CLIM1 (lower and upper limits of the confidence intervals), and PLIM and PLIM1 (for lower and upper limits of the prediction intervals). These are shown in Table 4.6. The columns in the table are labeled differently for clarity. The fitted value, confidence and prediction intervals are labeled as Fit, 95% CI and 95% PI.

Sample Calculation for Confidence Interval

Suppose we want to calculate a 95% confidence interval for the average value of y when $x = 951$. The regression equation for this problem is:

$$\hat{y} = b_0 + b_1 x$$

The predicted value $\hat{y}$ for $x = 951$ can be calculated as shown:

$$\hat{y} = 6.62 + 0.00964(951) = 15.79$$

(shown as 15.7874 in the column labeled Fit; the underlined row in Table 4.6). We can now calculate the confidence interval using the following equation:

$$\hat{y} \pm t_{\alpha/2, n-2}(s)\sqrt{\frac{1}{n} + \frac{(x_0 - \bar{x})^2}{\sum x^2 - \frac{(\sum x)^2}{n}}}$$

In the previous equation, $t_{\alpha/2,(n-2)} = t_{0.025,28} = 2.0484$ (from the t-table), $S_y = 0.1038$ and

$$\hat{y} = 15.7874 \text{ for } x = 951.$$

Therefore, the confidence interval for $x = 951$ is calculated as:

$$15.7874 - 2.0484\ (0.1038) \le \mu_{y|x_0} \le 15.7874 + 2.0484\ (0.1038) \text{ or}$$

$$15.5748 \le \mu_{y|x_0} \le 16.0000$$

This confidence interval means that we are 95% confident that the average number of hours required to produce 951 units is between 15.57 and 16.00 hours. The confidence interval calculated by MINITAB is underlined in Table 4.6. The program calculates the confidence intervals for all the x values in data. If the confidence intervals are desired for other values, they can be specified in the program.

Prediction Intervals

Generally, a prediction interval is calculated for a given value of x denoted by y_{x_0}. The interval is not referred to as confidence interval because y_{x_0} is a random variable and not a parameter.

Sample Calculation for Prediction Interval

Suppose we want to calculate a prediction interval for the predicted value of y for $x = 951$ units. This prediction of y can be calculated as:

$$\hat{y} = 6.62 + 0.00964x$$

$$= 6.62 + 0.00964 \, (951) = 15.79 \text{ hours}$$

(see the underlined row and the column labeled **Fit** in Table 4.6. The number is 15.7874).

The aforementioned is a prediction of a future value y for a given value of x, that is y_{x_0}. The $(1 - \alpha)$ 100% prediction interval for a future predicted value can be calculated using the equation:

$$\hat{y} - t_{\alpha/2,n-2}s_y \leq y_{x_0} \leq \hat{y} + t_{\alpha/2,n-2}s_y \text{ where,}$$

$$S_y = s\sqrt{1 + \frac{1}{n} + \frac{(x_0 - \bar{x})^2}{SS_x}}$$

The 95% prediction level for $x = 951$ is shown in Table 4.6 under 95% PI column and the underlined row. The prediction intervals for other predicted values are also calculated in this table and are shown under column **95.0% PI**.

Table 4.6 Fits, standard deviation of fits, confidence and prediction intervals (CI and PI)

Fit	StDev Fit	95.0% CI	95.0% PI
15.6042	0.0990	(15.4015, 15.8070)	(14.6639, 16.5445)
15.7874	0.1038	(15.5746, 16.0001)	(14.8449, 16.7299)
11.7391	0.1446	(11.4428, 12.0354)	(10.7743, 12.7039)
14.0042	0.0835	(13.8331, 14.1753)	(13.0702, 14.9382)
14.4669	0.0819	(14.2990, 14.6347)	(13.5335, 15.4003)
15.4307	0.0948	(15.2366, 15.6249)	(14.4923, 16.3692)
15.2862	0.0916	(15.0984, 15.4739)	(14.3490, 16.2233)
11.7776	0.1432	(11.4843, 12.0710)	(10.8137, 12.7416)
11.9608	0.1365	(11.6812, 12.2404)	(11.0010, 12.9206)
10.9102	0.1768	(10.5478, 11.2725)	(9.9231, 11.8972)
13.4066	0.0928	(13.2165, 13.5967)	(12.4689, 14.3443)
15.2669	0.0912	(15.0799, 15.4538)	(14.3299, 16.2039)
15.7681	0.1033	(15.5564, 15.9798)	(14.8258, 16.7104)
12.7126	0.1111	(12.4849, 12.9403)	(11.7666, 13.6586)
11.2186	0.1646	(10.8814, 11.5558)	(10.2404, 12.1968)
13.8885	0.0847	(13.7150, 14.0621)	(12.9541, 14.8230)
14.5151	0.0821	(14.3469, 14.6832)	(13.5816, 15.4485)
14.9970	0.0865	(14.8197, 15.1743)	(14.0619, 15.9321)
16.5970	0.1297	(16.3314, 16.8627)	(15.6412, 17.5529)
12.8476	0.1071	(12.6281, 13.0670)	(11.9035, 13.7916)
16.7898	0.1365	(16.5100, 17.0696)	(15.8300, 17.7497)
15.0548	0.0874	(14.8757, 15.2339)	(14.1193, 15.9903)
15.9609	0.1089	(15.7378, 16.1839)	(15.0160, 16.9058)
16.9826	0.1436	(16.6883, 17.2769)	(16.0184, 17.9468)
12.9343	0.1046	(12.7200, 13.1486)	(11.9914, 13.8772)
17.4645	0.1620	(17.1326, 17.7965)	(16.4882, 18.4409)
15.8741	0.1063	(15.6563, 16.0919)	(14.9305, 16.8178)
14.4765	0.0819	(14.3086, 14.6444)	(13.5431, 15.4099)
11.9704	0.1361	(11.6915, 12.2493)	(11.0108, 12.9300)
15.5368	0.0973	(15.3375, 15.7361)	(14.5972, 16.4763)

$\hat{y}$ s_y

Plotting the Confidence Intervals and Prediction Intervals

It is sometimes convenient to plot the confidence and prediction intervals along with the fitted line plot. Figure 4.2 shows such a plot. The plot was created using MINITAB. The instructions can be found in *Appendix A_ Table A.5*.

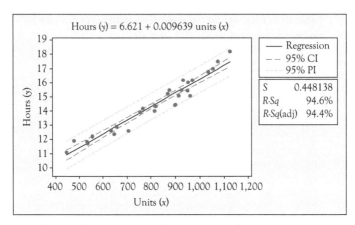

Figure 4.2 Confidence and prediction intervals

In Figure 4.2, the outermost bands are prediction intervals, and the inner bands are confidence intervals. The solid line is the fitted line of regression. From this figure, we can see that the width of prediction interval increases as the value of x increases or decreases from $\bar{x}$. It has a minimum width at $x = \bar{x}$. In general, the width of the prediction interval is always wider than the width of the confidence interval.

Assumptions of Regression Model

In linear regression analysis, the relationship between the dependent variable (y) to the independent variable (x) is assumed to be a model of the form $y = \beta_0 + \beta_1 x + \varepsilon$. This is a population model in which β_0 and β_1 are the parameters of the model and ε is the random error term.

The unknown population parameters β_0 and β_1 are estimated using the sample data. The estimates of β_0 and β_1 are denoted by b_0 and b_1 that provide the **estimated regression equation** given by the equation:

$$\hat{y} = b_0 + b_1 x$$

where $\hat{y}$ = point estimator of $E(y)$ or the mean value of y for a given value of x

b_0 = y-intercept of the regression line

b_1 = slope of the regression line

The preceding equation is the estimated line of regression in the slope intercept form. As discussed earlier, the y-intercept b_0 and the slope b_1 are determined using the **least squares method** that minimizes the sum of the square of the errors. The assumed regression model: $y = \beta_0 + \beta_1 x + \varepsilon$ is based on the following assumptions about the error ε.

1. The **independence of errors** assumption. This means that the individual values of the error terms, ε are independent of each other. That is, the error for a particular value of x is independent of any other value of x, or the value y for a given value of x is independent of the value of y for any other value of x. This assumption is critical when the data are collected over different time periods. When the data are collected over time, the errors in one time period may be correlated with another time period.

2. The **normality assumption**. This means that the errors (ε_i) are normally distributed at each value of x. Note that for a given value of x, there may be several values of y leading to several values of error ε. The distribution of errors ε_i for any value of x is normal.

   The normality assumption in regression is fairly robust against departures from normality. Unless the distribution of errors at each level of x is extremely different from normal, the inferences about the regression parameters β_0 and β_1 are not affected seriously.

3. The **population regression model**. The mean values of the dependent variable y for a given value of the independent variable x is the expected or the mean value of y denoted by $E(y)$ and is the population regression model given by: $E(y) + \beta_0 + \beta_1 x$.

   The expected values of y fall on the same straight line described by the model $E(y) + \beta_0 + \beta_1 x$. The mean value $E(y)$ is also written as $\mu_{y|x}$.

4. **Equality of variance assumption**. This assumption requires that the variance of the errors (ε_i), denoted by σ^2 are constant for all values of x. This means that the variability of y values is the same for low or high values of x. In case of serious departure from the equality of variance assumption, methods such as weighted least squares or data transformation may be used.

5. ***Linearity assumption.*** Besides the previous assumptions, one basic
assumption regarding the relationship between x and y is the ***linearity*** assumption, which means that the relationship between the two
variables is linear. The linearity assumption can be verified using a
residual plot to be discussed later. The assumptions are explained in
Figure 4.3.

Figure 4.3 illustrates the assumptions 2, 3, and 4. In this figure, the
regression model $E(y) = \beta_0 + \beta_1 x$ is shown using a straight line. This line
connects the average values of y or $E(y)$ for each specified value of the
independent variable x. Note that the $E(y)$ value changes for a specified
value of x but for each level of x, the probability distribution of error term
ε and the distribution of y-values for a given x are normally distributed
each with the same variance.

The assumption regarding the ***independence of errors*** can be evaluated by plotting the errors or residuals in the order or the sequence in
which the data were collected. If the errors are not independent, a relationship exists between consecutive residuals, which is a violation of the
assumption of independence of errors. When the errors are not independent, the plot of residuals versus the time (or the order) in which the data
were collected will show a cyclical pattern. Meeting this assumption is
particularly important when data are collected over a period of time. If
the data are collected at different time periods, the errors for specific time

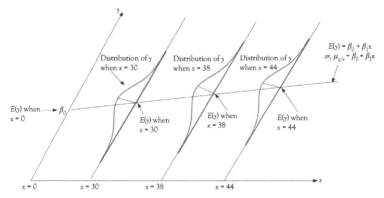

Figure 4.3 Illustration of linear regression model assumptions

Note: Distributions of y have the same shape for each value of x.

period may be correlated with the errors of those of the previous time periods.

The assumption that the errors are normally distributed, or the **normality assumption** requires that the errors have a normal or approximately normal distribution. Note that this assumption means that the errors do not deviate too much from normality. The assumption can be verified by plotting the histogram or the normal probability plot of errors.

The assumption regarding the mean value of y states that the means, $E(y)$ or $\mu_{y|x}$ all lie on the same straight line given by the population regression model: $E(y) + \beta_0 + \beta_1 x$.

The assumption that the variance of errors are equal (**equality of variance**) is also known as **homoscedasticity**. This requires that the errors are constant for all values of x or the variability of y values is the same for both the low and high values of x. The equality of variance assumption is of particular importance for making inferences about b_0 and b_1.

The **linearity** assumption means that the relationship between the variables is linear. This assumption can be verified using the residual plot, which will be discussed in the next section.

To check the validity of the preceding regression assumptions, a graphical approach known as the **residual analysis** is used. The residual analysis is also used to determine whether the selected regression model is an appropriate one.

Checking the Adequacy of the Regression Model: Residual Analysis

Before we conduct a residual analysis, we suggest a review of the residuals or errors discussed earlier. In this section, we will show how to use MINITAB to calculate the residuals and perform residual analysis.

Residuals: A residual or error for any point is the difference between the actual y value and the corresponding estimated value (denoted by y-cap, $\hat{y}$). Thus, for a given value of x, the residual is given by:

$$e = (y_i - \hat{y})$$

Calculating and Storing Residuals and Standardized Residuals Using MINITAB

The residuals can be easily computed using Excel or MINITAB. Table 4.7 shows values of **Fits**, **Residuals**, and **Standardized** residuals calculated using **MINITAB**. The instructions for computing this table is shown in *Appendix A _Table A.6.*

Here we demonstrate the calculations of residuals in Table 4.4. Suppose we want to calculate the residuals for the points ($x = 932, y = 16.20$) and ($x = 914, y = 15.08$). These are the first two values in the original data. The estimated equation of the regression line as reported on the session window should be:

$$\hat{y} = 6.62 + 0.00964x$$

for $x = 932$ $\qquad\qquad \hat{y} = 6.62 + 0.00964(932) = 15.6042$

which is the estimated value of y at $x = 932$. This is shown under the **FITS1** column in Table 4.7. Also, at $x = 932$, the observed value (actual data) of y is 16.20, therefore the *residual* or the *error* for ($x = 932$, $y = 16.20$) is $(y - \hat{y}) = (16.20 - 15.6042) = 0.5958$.

Using a similar approach, it can be verified that the residual ($x = 914$, $y = 15.08$) is -0.3507 (see Table 4.7). A negative value of the residual means that the observed point is below the fitted line; a positive residual indicates that the observed y is above the fitted line of regression. The residual for $x = 932$ is shown graphically in Figure 4.4.

The standardized residuals (**SRES1**) shown in the last column of Table 4.7 are calculated using the expression:

$$\frac{e_i}{\sqrt{MSE}}; i = 1, 2, \ldots, n \qquad (4.2)$$

where e_i is the residual for point i and n is the number of observations, and MSE is the mean square error from the ANOVA table of regression output (see analysis of variance part of Table 4.5).

Table 4.7 Residuals and standardized residuals

Row	Units(x)	Hours(y)	FITS1	RESI1	SRES1
1	932	16.20	15.6042	0.595759	1.36306
2	951	16.05	15.7874	0.262623	0.60243
3	531	11.84	11.7391	0.100907	0.23790
4	766	14.21	14.0042	0.205796	0.46741
5	814	14.42	14.4669	-0.046866	-0.10637
6	914	15.08	15.4307	-0.350743	-0.80077
7	899	14.45	15.2862	-0.836161	1.90613
8	535	11.73	11.7776	-0.047648	-0.11221
9	554	12.24	11.9608	0.279215	0.65413
10	445	11.12	10.9102	0.209841	0.50961
11	704	12.63	13.4066	-0.776601	-1.77135
12	897	14.43	15.2669	-0.836884	-1.90743
13	949	15.46	15.7681	-0.308100	-0.70654
14	632	12.64	12.7126	-0.072609	-0.16725
15	477	11.92	11.2186	0.701401	1.68275
16	754	13.95	13.8885	0.061461	0.13967
17	819	14.33	14.5151	-0.185059	-0.42006
18	869	15.23	14.9970	0.233002	0.52991
19	1035	16.77	16.5970	0.172966	0.40321
20	646	12.41	12.8476	-0.437552	-1.00551
21	1055	17.00	16.7898	0.210190	0.49245
22	875	15.50	15.0548	0.445169	1.01283
23	969	16.20	15.9609	0.239125	0.55007
24	1075	17.50	16.9826	0.517415	1.21888
25	655	12.92	12.9343	-0.014301	-0.03282
26	1125	18.20	17.4645	0.735476	1.76026
27	960	15.10	15.8741	-0.774126	-1.77818
28	815	14.00	14.4765	-0.476504	-1.08153
29	555	12.20	11.9704	0.229576	0.53770
30	925	15.50	15.5368	-0.036769	-0.08405
	$\updownarrow$	$\updownarrow$	$\updownarrow$	$\updownarrow$	$\updownarrow$
	x	y	$\hat{y}$	$(y - \hat{y})$	
			Fits	Residuals	Standardized Residuals

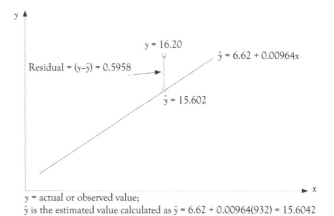

y = actual or observed value;
$\hat{y}$ is the estimated value calculated as $\hat{y}$ = 6.62 + 0.00964(932) = 15.6042

Figure 4.4 Calculation of residuals

The sum of the residuals is always zero. We can see in Figure 4.4, the residual is the vertical distance from the fitted line of regression to the observed data point. The estimated least squares regression line is the "best" fit line through all of the data points. Therefore, the vertical distances from the estimated line to the points will cancel each other and the sum of the residuals would be zero. This can be verified by adding the residual (RESI1) column in Table 4.7.

Checking the Assumptions of Regression Using MINITAB Residual Plots

Several residual plots can be created using Excel and MINITAB to check the adequacy of the regression model. The instructions for creating residuals plots are shown in **Appendix A_Table A.7**. The plots are shown in Figure 4.5(a) through (d).

The plots to check the regression assumptions include the histogram of residuals, normal plot of residuals, plot of the residuals versus fits, and residuals versus order of data. The residuals can also be plotted with each of the independent variables.

Figure 4.5(a) and (b) are used to check the normality assumption. The regression model assumes that the errors are normally distributed with mean zero. Figure 4.5(a) shows the normal probability plot. This plot is

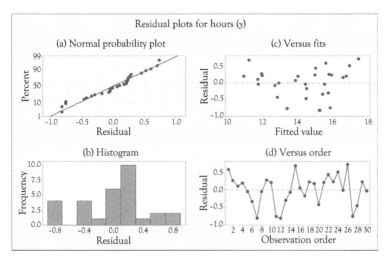

Figure 4.5 Plots for residual analysis

used to check for the normality assumption of regression model. In this plot, if the plotted points lie on a straight line or close to a straight line, then the residuals or errors are normally distributed. The pattern of points appear to fall on a straight line, indicating no violation of the normality assumption.

Figure 4.5(b) shows the histogram of residuals. If the normality assumption holds, the histogram of residuals should look symmetrical or approximately symmetrical. Also, the histogram should be centered at zero because the sum of the residuals is always zero. The histogram of residuals is approximately symmetrical, which indicates that the errors appear to be approximately normally distributed. Note that the histogram may not be exactly symmetrical. We would like to see a pattern that is symmetrical or approximately symmetrical.

In Figure 4.5(c), the residuals are plotted against the fitted value and the order of the data points. These plots are used to check the assumptions of linearity. The points in this plot should be scattered randomly around the horizontal line drawn through the zero residual value for the linear model to be valid. As can be seen, the residuals are randomly scattered about the horizontal line, indicating that the relationship between x and y is linear.

The plot of residual versus the order of the data shown in Figure 4.5(d) is used to check the independence of errors. The independence of errors can be checked by plotting the errors or the residuals in the order or sequence in which the data were collected. The plot of residuals versus the order of data should show no pattern or apparent relationship between the consecutive residuals. This plot shows no apparent pattern indicating that the assumption of independence of errors is not violated. Note that checking the independence of errors is more important in cases where the data were collected over time. Data collected over time sometimes may show an autocorrelation effect among successive data values. In these cases, there may be a relationship between consecutive residuals that violates the assumption of independence of errors.

The equality of variance assumption requires that the errors are constant for all values of x or the variability of y is the same for both the low and high values of x. This can be checked by plotting the residuals and the order of data points. This plot is shown in Figure 4.5(d). If the equality of variance assumption is violated, this plot will show an increasing trend showing an increasing variability. This demonstrates a lack of homogeneity in the variances of y values at each level of x. The plot shows no violation of equality of variance assumption.

Test for Outliers and Influential Observations in Simple Regression

Outliers are the points with large x or y values or both, and they affect the fitted line of regression and the overall model. The fitted regression line is pulled in the direction of an outlier. They generally do not fit with the rest of the data and may have a strong impact on correlation, coefficient of determination, and other statistics. The outliers may produce large errors affecting the overall prediction ability of the regression model. The outlier may be detected through the visual observation of points on the scatter plot, but sometimes more formal analysis is required. These points should be detected and their cause or causes investigated so that the points may be removed or corrected to improve the overall effectiveness of the model.

In regression analysis, we are interested in determining how influential the outliers are in estimating the regression line. *Influential points* are those points whose removal will cause a shift in the regression line. Several statistical packages, including MINITAB, provide computations to study the outlier effect or the *influence* of each of the points on the fitted regression line. This is also called *Influence Analysis*. We will consider the following:

1. Sample leverages [H_i (**leverages**)] to identify the outlying values of the independent variable x.
2. **Standardized residuals** to identify the outlying values of the dependent variable y.
3. **Cook's distance** to identify the influential observations.

The previous values are shown in Table 4.8. The table is generated using MINITAB (the instructions can be found in *Appendix A_Table A.8*. The table shows the values [**Units (x)** and **Hours (y)**], **FITS1** (Fits), **RESI1** (residuals), **SRES1** (standardized residuals), **HI1** (leverages), and **COOK1** (Cook's distance). We will discuss these columns in our further analysis of outliers. First, we will discuss the leverages (HI1) column, then the standardized residuals (SRES1) followed by the Cook's distance (COOK1). These values are used to detect the outlier and influential points.

(1) H_i (Leverages)

The H_i or the leverages are used to determine extremely large or small values of the independent variable x that may have an effect on the regression line. The large or the small values of h_i are based on the distances of the x or independent values from the mean $\bar{x}$. The leverage h_i of the ith observation is given by:

$$h_i = \frac{1}{n} + \frac{(x_i - \bar{x})}{\sum x^2 - \frac{(\sum x)^2}{n}} \qquad (4.3)$$

The leverages are calculated and stored as H_i in MINITAB. To determine whether an independent variable x is an outlier or not, the following decision rule is used:

If the leverage $H_i > 6/n$ for a given independent variable x then that value of x is an outlier.

Note that n is the number of observations. In our example, $n = 30$ so $6/n = 6/30 = 0.2$. This means that any H value larger than 0.2 would be considered an outlier. Table 4.8 shows the leverages H_i (labeled **HI1**) for our example. If you look into the column labeled **HI1**, none of the values are greater than 0.2, which indicates that there are no extremely large or small x values or outliers.

(2) SRES1 (Standardized Residuals)

The other column of interest in Table 4.8 is SRES1 or standardized residuals column. The standardized residuals are used to detect unusually large or small values of dependent variable y. The standardized residuals are calculated using the following formula:

$$SRES1 = \frac{y - \hat{y}}{s\sqrt{(1 - h_i)}} \qquad (4.4)$$

where $(y - \hat{y})$ = residual, s = standard error of the estimate ($s = 0.4481$ for our example), h_i is given by Equation 4.3. Suppose we want to calculate the standardized residual for the 20th point in Table 4.8 where $x = 646$ and $y = 12.41$. For row number 20, we have HI1= 0.057106, and $(y - \hat{y})$, which is the residual or RESI1 = -0.437552, and $S = 0.4481$. Substituting these values in Equation 4.4 gives the value of standardized residual = -1.00551 (see row 20 and column labeled SRES1 in Table 4.8). The other values of standardized residuals are calculated in a similar way.

As indicated earlier, the standardized residuals are used to detect the outlying value of the dependent variable y. The following decision rule is applied to detect the outlying value of y:

If the standardized residual value (SRES1 column in Table 4.8) for any y value is larger than +2 or smaller than −2, then that value y would be considered an outlier.

An examination of the SRES1 column of Table 4.8, where the standardized residuals are stored, shows that none of the values are greater than +2 or less than −2, therefore, we will conclude that there are no outlying y values in this case.

(3) COOK1 (Cook's Distance)

The Cook's distance (column labeled **COOK1** in Table 4.8) is used to detect the influential points in the model. An influential point is one that has a great impact on the fitted line of regression and the removal of which would result in a change in the slope b_1 and y-intercept b_0 of the fitted line.

The Cook's distance combines the leverage value h_i and the standardized residual value together to provide a single measure that can be used to detect the influential points in the model. Recall that the leverage value h_i detects the outlying x value and the standardized residual detects the outlying y value. The outliers detected by either measures may not be influential points (i.e., their removal may or may not have an impact on the fitted line of regression). The Cook's distance provides a more reliable measure for the detection of influential points. It is calculated using the following expression:

$$D_i = \frac{1}{2}\frac{h_i}{(1 - h_i)}(SRES)^2 \qquad (4.5)$$

Table 4.8 Calculated values for analysis of outlier

Row	Units (x)	Hours (y)	FITS1	RESI1	SRES1	HI1	COOK1
1	932	16.20	15.6042	0.595759	1.36306	0.048760	0.047618
2	951	16.05	15.7874	0.262623	0.60243	0.053696	0.010297
3	531	11.84	11.7391	0.100907	0.23790	0.104155	0.003290
4	766	14.21	14.0042	0.205796	0.46741	0.034730	0.003930
5	814	14.42	14.4669	-0.046866	-0.10637	0.033421	0.000196
6	914	15.08	15.4307	-0.350743	-0.80077	0.044715	0.015007
7	899	14.45	15.2862	-0.836161	-1.90613	0.041812	0.079274
8	535	11.73	11.7776	-0.047648	-0.11221	0.102097	0.000716
9	554	12.24	11.9608	0.279215	0.65413	0.092740	0.021869
10	445	11.12	10.9102	0.209841	0.50961	0.155717	0.023949
11	704	12.63	13.4066	-0.776601	-1.77135	0.042884	0.070292
12	897	14.43	15.2669	-0.836884	-1.90743	0.041458	0.078679
13	949	15.46	15.7681	-0.308100	-0.70654	0.053144	0.014009
14	632	12.64	12.7126	-0.072609	-0.16725	0.061494	0.000916
15	477	11.92	11.2186	0.701401	1.68275	0.134894	0.220766
16	754	13.95	13.8885	0.061461	0.13967	0.035740	0.000362
17	819	14.33	14.5151	-0.185059	-0.42006	0.033535	0.003061
18	869	15.23	14.9970	0.233002	0.52991	0.037287	0.005438
19	1035	16.77	16.5970	0.172966	0.40321	0.083716	0.007427
20	646	12.41	12.8476	-0.437552	-1.00551	0.057106	0.030617
21	1055	17.00	16.7898	0.210190	0.49245	0.092835	0.012408
22	875	15.50	15.0548	0.445169	1.01283	0.038056	0.020292
23	969	16.20	15.9609	0.239125	0.55007	0.059003	0.009486
24	1075	17.50	16.9826	0.517415	1.21888	0.102711	0.085031
25	655	12.92	12.9343	-0.014301	-0.03282	0.054481	0.000031
26	1125	18.20	17.4645	0.735476	1.76026	0.130719	0.232970
27	960	15.10	15.8741	-0.774126	-1.77818	0.056273	0.094271
28	815	14.00	14.4765	-0.476504	-1.08153	0.033440	0.020234
29	555	12.20	11.9704	0.229576	0.53770	0.092266	0.014694
30	925	15.50	15.5368	-0.036769	-0.08405	0.047114	0.000175
	↕	↕	↕	↕	↕	↕	↕
	x	y	$\hat{y}$	$(y - \hat{y})$ Residuals	Standardized Residuals	Leverage	Cook's Distance

where, h_i are the leverage values and SRES are the standardized residuals. The standardized residuals are calculated using Equation 4.4. Therefore, substituting into Equation 4.5 we get:

$$D_i = \frac{(Y_i - \hat{Y})^2 h_i}{2s^2 (1 - h_i)^2} \tag{4.6}$$

Equation 4.6 can be used to calculate the Cook's distance for any point. For example, suppose we want to calculate the Cook's distance for point 20 in Table 4.8. For this point, $y = 12.41$, $\hat{y} = 12.8476$, (under **FIT** column), $h_i = 0.057106$ (under HI column), and $s = 0.4481$ (from regression analysis Table 4.5). Substituting the preceding values in Equation 4.6, we get:

$$D_i = \frac{(12.41 - 12.8476)^2 (0.057106)}{2(0.4481)^2 (1 - 0.057106)^2} = 0.03062$$

which is close to the value in the row under COOK1 column. The Cook's distance for all the other points are calculated and reported under the COOK1 column of Table 4.8. The decision rule to detect an influential point using the Cook's distance is given as:

If the Cook's distance $D_i > 0.8$ for a given point, then the point is an influential point.

An examination of COOK1 column of Table 4.8 shows that, for our example, none of the distances are larger than 0.8. This indicates that none of the points are influential.

The Durbin–Watson Statistic: Measuring and Checking Autocorrelation in Regression

One of the basic assumptions of regression analysis is that the errors are independent. This assumption is sometimes violated if the data are collected over sequential time period. *Data collected over time sometimes show an autocorrelation effect among successive data values. In such cases, there will be a relationship between consecutive residuals that violates the assumption of independence of errors.*

The autocorrelation effect among successive observations can be tested using the Durbin–Watson statistic.

Durbin–Watson statistic

The Durbin–Watson statistic tests the autocorrelation. The null hypothesis using the Durbin–Watson statistic is that the residuals from an ordinary least squares regression are not autocorrelated. In other words, it is a test performed to determine whether the residuals from a linear or multiple regression are independent. Regression analysis using time series data (data collected over time) usually exhibit positive autocorrelation that violates the independence of error assumption of regression. The steps for the test are explained as follows:

Step 1: State the null and alternate hypotheses.

The hypothesis for Durbin–Watson test can be stated as:

$$H_0 : \rho = 0 \text{ (residuals are not autocorrelated)}$$
$$H_1 : \rho > 0 \text{ (residuals are autocorrelated)}$$

(4.7)

Step 2: Specify the test statistic.

The test statistic for the test is given by:

$$d = \frac{\sum\limits_{i=2}^{n}(e_i - e_{i-1})^2}{\sum\limits_{i=1}^{n} e_i^2} \qquad (4.8)$$

where e_i is the residual given by $e_i = y_i - \hat{y}$; the difference between the observed and predicted values for the ith value of the response variable. Note that the value of the test statistic d becomes smaller as the serial correlations increase.

Step 3: Calculate the test statistic value.

Calculating the value of the Durbin–Watson Statistic d using Equation (4.8)

We will use the example problem (Table 3.1_Chapter 3) or the data file: **Hours_Units** to test the hypothesis stated in Equation 4.7. First, we calculate the Durbin–Watson statistic (d) using Equation 4.8. To calculate d, the residuals are calculated using MINITAB (instructions in (*Appendix A_Table A.9*). Once the residuals are known, the statistic d can be calculated as shown in Table 4.9.

Step 4: Determine the critical values for the test using Durbin–Watson statistical table.

Durbin–Watson Statistical Table

Upper and lower critical values of the test statistic $d - d_U$ and d_L have been tabulated for different values of k (the number of explanatory or independent variables) and n (the number of observations) in Durbin–Watson statistic table (Table 4.10). This table can be used to test the hypothesis in Equation 4.7.

Critical values: The lower and upper critical points, d_L and d_U are obtained from Table 4.10. Refer to this table for the number of observations (n) and the number of independent variables (k) in the example. For our example, $n = 30$ and $k = 1$, the corresponding values are:

$$d_L = 1.352 \text{ and } d_U = 1.489$$

Table 4.9 Calculation of Durbin–Watson statistic, d

Row	Unit (x)	Hours (y)	Residuals (e_i-e_{i-1})	(e_i-e_{i-1})	$(e_i-e_{i-1})^2$	e_i^2
1	932	16.20	0.595759	*	*	0.35493
2	951	16.05	0.262623	0.33314	0.11098	0.06897
3	531	11.84	0.100907	0.16172	0.02615	0.01018
4	766	14.21	0.205796	-0.10489	0.01100	0.04235
5	814	14.42	-0.046866	0.25266	0.06384	0.00220
6	914	15.08	-0.350743	0.30388	0.09234	0.12302
7	899	14.45	-0.836161	0.48542	0.23563	0.69917
8	535	11.73	-0.047648	-0.78851	0.62175	0.00227
9	554	12.24	0.279215	-0.32686	0.10684	0.07796
10	445	11.12	0.209841	0.06937	0.00481	0.04403
11	704	12.63	-0.776601	0.98644	0.97307	0.60311
12	897	14.43	-0.836884	0.06028	0.00363	0.70037
13	949	15.46	-0.308100	-0.52878	0.27961	0.09493
14	632	12.64	-0.072609	-0.23549	0.05546	0.00527
15	477	11.92	0.701401	-0.77401	0.59909	0.49196
16	754	13.95	0.061461	0.63994	0.40952	0.00378
17	819	14.33	-0.185059	0.24652	0.06077	0.03425
18	869	15.23	0.233002	-0.41806	0.17478	0.05429
19	1035	16.77	0.172966	0.06004	0.00360	0.02992
20	646	12.41	-0.437552	0.61052	0.37273	0.19145
21	1055	17.00	0.210190	-0.64774	0.41957	0.04418
22	875	15.50	0.445169	-0.23498	0.05522	0.19818
23	969	16.20	0.239125	0.20604	0.04245	0.05718
24	1075	17.50	0.517415	-0.27829	0.07745	0.26772
25	655	12.92	-0.014301	0.53172	0.28272	0.00020
26	1125	18.20	0.735476	-0.74978	0.56217	0.54093
27	960	15.10	-0.774126	1.50960	2.27890	0.59927
28	815	14.00	-0.476504	-0.29762	0.08858	0.22706
29	555	12.20	0.229576	-0.70608	0.49855	0.05271
30	925	15.50	-0.036769	0.26635	0.07094	0.00135

$$\sum_{i=2}^{n} (e_i-e_{i-1})^2 = 8.58216 \qquad \sum_{i=1}^{n} e_i^2 = 5.62318$$

$$d = \frac{\sum_{i=2}^{n} (e_i-e_{i-1})^2}{\sum_{i=1}^{n} e_i^2} = \frac{8.58216}{5.62318} = 1.5262$$

Step 5: Specify the decision rule. The decision rule is given by:

If $d < d_L$; reject $H_0 : \rho = 0$ (indicating evidence of autocorrelation)
If $d > d_U$; do not reject $H_0 : \rho = 0$ (indicating no evidence of autocorrelation)
If $d_L < d < d_U$ (test is inconclusive)   (4.9)

Step 6: Make a decision and state your conclusion.
The computed value, $d = 1.5262$ (see Table 4.9), is greater than d_U (=1.489); therefore, do not reject H_0 and conclude that there is no evidence of autocorrelation.

Table 4.10 Durbin–Watson statistic table of d_L and d_U at 5% significance level (k is the number of independent variables and n = number of observations)

n	k=1		k=2		k=3		k=4		k=5		k=6		k=7	
	dL	dU	dL	dU	dL	dU	dL	dU	dL	dU	dL	dU	dL	dU
6	0.610	1.400												
7	0.700	1.356	0.467	1.896										
8	0.763	1.332	0.559	1.777	0.368	2.287								
9	0.824	1.320	0.629	1.699	0.455	2.128	0.296	2.588						
10	0.879	1.320	0.697	1.641	0.525	2.016	0.376	2.414	0.243	2.822				
11	0.927	1.324	0.758	1.604	0.595	1.928	0.444	2.283	0.316	2.645	0.203	3.005		
12	0.971	1.331	0.812	1.579	0.658	1.864	0.512	2.177	0.379	2.506	0.268	2.832	0.171	3.149
13	1.010	1.340	0.861	1.562	0.715	1.816	0.574	2.094	0.445	2.390	0.328	2.692	0.230	2.985
14	1.045	1.350	0.905	1.551	0.767	1.779	0.632	2.030	0.505	2.296	0.389	2.572	0.286	2.848
15	1.077	1.361	0.946	1.543	0.814	1.750	0.685	1.977	0.562	2.220	0.447	2.472	0.343	2.727
16	1.106	1.371	0.982	1.539	0.857	1.728	0.734	1.935	0.615	2.157	0.502	2.388	0.398	2.624
17	1.133	1.381	1.015	1.536	0.897	1.710	0.779	1.900	0.664	2.104	0.554	2.318	0.451	2.537
18	1.158	1.391	1.046	1.535	0.933	1.696	0.820	1.872	0.710	2.060	0.603	2.257	0.502	2.461
19	1.180	1.401	1.074	1.536	0.967	1.685	0.859	1.848	0.752	2.023	0.649	2.206	0.549	2.396
20	1.201	1.411	1.100	1.537	0.998	1.676	0.894	1.828	0.792	1.991	0.692	2.162	0.595	2.339
21	1.221	1.420	1.125	1.538	1.026	1.669	0.927	1.812	0.829	1.964	0.732	2.124	0.637	2.290
22	1.239	1.429	1.147	1.541	1.053	1.664	0.958	1.797	0.863	1.940	0.769	2.090	0.677	2.246
23	1.257	1.437	1.168	1.543	1.078	1.660	0.986	1.785	0.895	1.920	0.804	2.061	0.715	2.208
24	1.273	1.446	1.188	1.546	1.101	1.656	1.013	1.775	0.925	1.902	0.837	2.035	0.751	2.174
25	1.288	1.454	1.206	1.550	1.123	1.654	1.038	1.767	0.953	1.886	0.868	2.012	0.784	2.144
26	1.302	1.461	1.224	1.553	1.143	1.652	1.062	1.759	0.979	1.873	0.897	1.992	0.816	2.117
27	1.316	1.469	1.240	1.556	1.162	1.651	1.084	1.753	1.004	1.861	0.925	1.974	0.845	2.093
28	1.328	1.476	1.255	1.560	1.181	1.650	1.104	1.747	1.028	1.850	0.951	1.958	0.874	2.071
29	1.341	1.483	1.270	1.563	1.198	1.650	1.124	1.743	1.050	1.841	0.975	1.944	0.900	2.052
30	1.352	1.489	1.284	1.567	1.214	1.650	1.143	1.739	1.071	1.833	0.998	1.931	0.926	2.034
31	1.363	1.496	1.297	1.570	1.229	1.650	1.160	1.735	1.090	1.825	1.020	1.920	0.950	2.018
32	1.373	1.502	1.309	1.574	1.244	1.650	1.177	1.732	1.109	1.819	1.041	1.909	0.972	2.004
33	1.383	1.508	1.321	1.577	1.258	1.651	1.193	1.730	1.127	1.813	1.061	1.900	0.994	1.991
34	1.393	1.514	1.333	1.580	1.271	1.652	1.208	1.728	1.144	1.808	1.080	1.891	1.015	1.979
35	1.402	1.519	1.343	1.584	1.283	1.652	1.222	1.726	1.160	1.803	1.097	1.884	1.034	1.967
36	1.411	1.525	1.354	1.587	1.295	1.654	1.236	1.724	1.175	1.799	1.114	1.877	1.053	1.957
37	1.419	1.530	1.364	1.590	1.307	1.655	1.249	1.723	1.190	1.795	1.131	1.870	1.071	1.948
38	1.427	1.535	1.373	1.594	1.318	1.656	1.261	1.722	1.204	1.792	1.146	1.864	1.088	1.939
39	1.435	1.540	1.382	1.597	1.328	1.658	1.273	1.722	1.218	1.789	1.161	1.859	1.104	1.932
40	1.442	1.544	1.391	1.600	1.338	1.659	1.285	1.721	1.230	1.786	1.175	1.854	1.120	1.924
45	1.475	1.566	1.430	1.615	1.383	1.666	1.336	1.720	1.287	1.776	1.238	1.835	1.189	1.895
50	1.503	1.585	1.462	1.628	1.421	1.674	1.378	1.721	1.335	1.771	1.291	1.822	1.246	1.875
55	1.528	1.601	1.490	1.641	1.452	1.681	1.414	1.724	1.374	1.768	1.334	1.814	1.294	1.861
60	1.549	1.616	1.514	1.652	1.480	1.689	1.444	1.727	1.408	1.767	1.372	1.808	1.335	1.850
65	1.567	1.629	1.536	1.662	1.503	1.696	1.471	1.731	1.438	1.767	1.404	1.805	1.370	1.843
70	1.583	1.641	1.554	1.672	1.525	1.703	1.494	1.735	1.464	1.768	1.433	1.802	1.401	1.837
75	1.598	1.652	1.571	1.680	1.543	1.709	1.515	1.739	1.487	1.770	1.458	1.801	1.428	1.834
80	1.611	1.662	1.586	1.688	1.560	1.715	1.534	1.743	1.507	1.772	1.480	1.801	1.453	1.831
85	1.624	1.671	1.600	1.696	1.575	1.721	1.550	1.747	1.525	1.774	1.500	1.801	1.474	1.829
90	1.635	1.679	1.612	1.703	1.589	1.726	1.566	1.751	1.542	1.776	1.518	1.801	1.494	1.827
95	1.645	1.687	1.623	1.709	1.602	1.732	1.579	1.755	1.557	1.778	1.535	1.802	1.512	1.827
100	1.654	1.694	1.634	1.715	1.613	1.736	1.592	1.758	1.571	1.780	1.550	1.803	1.528	1.826
150	1.720	1.746	1.706	1.760	1.693	1.774	1.679	1.788	1.665	1.802	1.651	1.817	1.637	1.832
200	1.758	1.778	1.748	1.789	1.738	1.799	1.728	1.810	1.718	1.820	1.707	1.831	1.697	1.841

Source: Savin and Kenneth (1977).

Summary

This chapter provided a detailed and stepwise computer analysis of the simple regression using Excel and MINITAB. Instructions were provided for running the simple regression using both these software and the computer results were explained. The Excel regression output is divided into two parts: *Regression Statistics* and *ANOVA*. The *Regression Statistics* part contains important measures such as *Multiple R, R-Square, Adjusted R-Square*, and *Standard Error*. These measures are important in assessing the regression model. The ANOVA table of the regression output contains the information to calculate the value of *R-Square*—the coefficient of determination, which is a measure of goodness of fit for the regression equation. The ANOVA table can be used to conduct the *F*-test for the significance of regression. Another test for the significance of regression—the t-test was also discussed.

A more detailed computer analysis was provided using the MINITAB statistical software. MINITAB provides more detailed analysis, including the visual representation wherever applicable. Among the key analysis features were: (a) creating and interpreting a scatter diagram; (b) constructing a fitted line plot, including the equation of the best fitting line; (c) interpreting the regression analysis and analysis of variance tables. Both these tables were explained in detail. In addition, we used MINITAB to calculate and interpret the following: (a) confidence interval for the slope of the fitted regression line, β_1 and (b) confidence and prediction intervals and their interpretation in simple linear regression. We provided a detailed discussion on residual analysis and discussed assumptions underlying the regression model. Finally, we discussed how the outliers influence the results of regression and provided tests for outliers and influential observations in simple regression. One of the considerations in simple regression is to check for autocorrelation effect. This can be checked using the Durbin–Watson statistic that allows us to measure and check the autocorrelation in regression. A computer analysis was presented for Durbin–Watson test.

CHAPTER 5

Multiple Regression: Computer Analysis

This chapter provides in-depth analysis of multiple regression model. This is one of the most widely used prediction techniques used in data analysis and decision making. Multiple regression enables us to explore the relationship between a response variable, and two or more independent variables or the predictors. The multiple regression model can be used to predict a response variable using two or more predictors or independent variables. In this chapter we will:

- Outline the difference between simple and multiple regression;
- Explain the multiple regression model and how to establish multiple regression equation;
- Use the multiple regression model to make inferences;
- Assess the quality of multiple regression model by calculating different measures;
- Interpret the computer results from computer packages, such as Excel and MINITAB;
- Test the hypotheses to assess the overall significance of multiple regression model (F-test);
- Test the hypotheses to determine whether each of the independent variables is significant (t-tests);
- Explain multicollinearity problem in multiple regression and explain how to detect multicollinearity;
- Outline the underlying assumptions of multiple regression; and
- Perform residual analysis to check whether the assumptions of multiple regression are met.

Introduction to Multiple Regression

In the previous chapter, we explored the relationship between two variables using simple regression and correlation analysis. We demonstrated how the estimated regression equation can be used to predict a dependent variable (y) using an independent variable (x). We also discussed the correlation between two variables that explains the degree of association between two variables. In this chapter, we expand the concept of simple linear regression to include multiple regression analysis. A multiple linear regression involves *one dependent or response* variable, and *two or more independent variables* or *predictors*. The concepts of simple regression discussed in the previous chapter are also applicable to the multiple regression.

Multiple Regression Model

The mathematical form of multiple linear regression model relating the dependent variable y and two or more independent variables x_1, x_2, ..., x_k with the associated error term is given by:

$$y = \beta_0 + \beta_1 x_1 + \beta_2 x_2 + \beta_3 x_3 + ... + \beta_k x_k + \varepsilon \qquad (5.1)$$

where x_1, x_2, ..., x_k are k independent or explanatory variables; β_0, β_1, β_2, ..., β_k are the regression coefficients, and ε is the associated error term. Equation 5.1 can be viewed as a **population multiple regression model** in which y is a linear function of unknown parameters β_0, β_1, β_2, ..., β_k and an error term, ε. The error ε explains the variability in y that cannot be explained by the linear effects of the independent variables. The multiple regression model is similar to the simple regression model except that multiple regression involves more than one independent variable.

One of the basic assumptions of the regression analysis is that the mean or the expected value of the error is zero. This implies that the mean or expected value of y or $E(y)$ in the multiple regression model can be given by:

$$E(y) = \beta_0 + \beta_1 x_1 + \beta_2 x_2 + \beta_3 x_3 + ... + \beta_k x_k \qquad (5.2)$$

Equation 5.2 relating the mean value of y and the k independent variables is known as the **multiple regression equation**.

It is important to note that $\beta_0, \beta_1, \beta_2, \ldots, \beta_k$ are the unknown population parameters, or regression coefficients, and they must be estimated using the sample data to obtain the estimated equation of multiple regression. The estimated regression coefficients are denoted by $b_0, b_1, b_2, \ldots, b_k$. These are the point estimates of the parameters $\beta_0, \beta_1, \beta_2, \ldots, \beta_k$. The estimated multiple regression equation using the estimates of the unknown population regression coefficients can be written as:

$$\hat{y} = b_0 + b_1 x_1 + b_2 x_2 + b_3 x_3 + \ldots + b_k x_k \qquad (5.3)$$

where $\hat{y}$ = point estimator of $E(y)$ or the estimated value of the response y, $b_0, b_1, b_2, \ldots, b_k$ are the estimated regression coefficients and are the estimates of $\beta_0, \beta_1, \beta_2, \ldots, \beta_k$.

Equation 5.3 is the **estimated multiple regression equation** and can be viewed as the sample regression model. This equation is written with sample regression coefficients. This equation defines the regression equation for k independent variables.

In Equation 5.1, $\beta_0, \beta_1, \beta_2, \ldots, \beta_k$ denote the regression coefficients for the population. The sample regression coefficients $b_0, b_1, b_2, \ldots, b_k$ are the estimates of the population parameters and can be determined using the **least squares** method.

In a multiple linear regression, the variation in y (the response variable) may be explained using two or more independent variables or predictors. The objective is to predict the dependent variable y. Compared to simple linear regression, a more precise prediction can be made because we use two or more independent variables. By using two or more independent variables, we are often able to make use of more information in the model. The simplest form of a multiple linear regression model involves two independent variables and can be written as:

$$y = \beta_0 + \beta_1 x_1 + \beta_2 x_2 + \varepsilon \qquad (5.4)$$

Equation 5.4 describes a plane. In this equation, β_0 is the y-intercept of the regression plane. The parameter β_1 indicates the average change in y for each unit change in x_1 when x_2 is constant. Similarly, β_2 indicates the average change in y for each unit change in x_2 when x_1 is held constant.

When we have more than two independent variables, the regression equation of the form described using Equation 5.3 is the equation of a *hyperplane* in an *n*-dimensional space.

The Least Squares Multiple Regression Model

The regression model is described in the form of a regression equation that is obtained using the **least squares method**. Recall that in a simple regression, *the least squares method requires fitting a line through the data points so that the sums of the squares of errors or residuals are minimized. These errors or residuals are the vertical distances of the points from the fitted line.* The same concept of simple regression is used to develop the multiple regression equation.

In a multiple regression, the least squares method determines the best-fitting plane or the hyperplane through the data points that ensures that the sum of the squares of the vertical distances or deviations from the given points and the plane are a minimum.

Figure 5.1 shows a multiple regression model with two independent variables. The response y with two independent variables x_1 and x_2 forms a regression plane. The observed data points in the figure are shown using dots. The stars on the regression plane indicate the corresponding points that have identical values for x_1 and x_2. The vertical distance from the observed points to the point on plane are shown using vertical lines. These

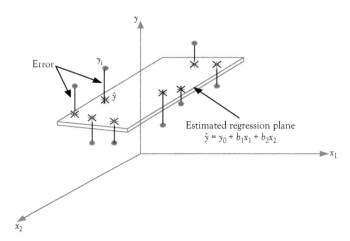

Figure 5.1 *Scatterplot and regression plane with two independent variables*

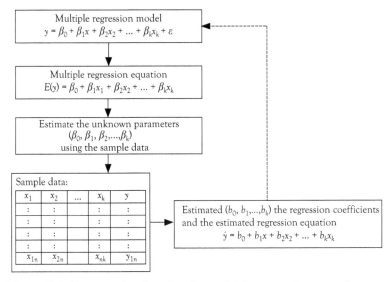

Figure 5.2 Process of estimating the multiple regression equation

vertical lines are the errors. The error for a particular point y_i is denoted by $(y_i - \hat{y})$ where the estimated value $\hat{y}$ is calculated using the regression equation: $\hat{y} = b_0 + b_1 x_1 + b_2 x_2$ for a given value of x_1 and x_2.

The least squares criteria requires that the sum of the squares of the errors be minimized, or,

$$\Sigma\, (y - \hat{y})^2$$

where y is the observed value and $\hat{y}$ is the estimated value of the dependent variable given by $\hat{y} = b_0 + b_1 x_1 + b_2 x_2$.

Similar to the simple regression, the least squares method uses the sample data to estimate the regression coefficients b_0, b_1, b_2, ..., b_k and hence the estimated equation of multiple regression. Figure 5.2 shows the process of estimating the regression coefficients and the multiple regression equation.

Models with Two Quantitative Independent Variables x_1 and x_2

The model with two quantitative independent variables is the simplest multiple regression model. It is a first-order model and is written as:

$$y = b_0 + b_1 x_1 + b_2 x_2 \qquad (5.5)$$

where, b_0 = y-intercept, the value of y when $x_1 = x_2 = 0$

b_1 = change in y for a 1-unit increase in x_1 when x_2 is constant

b_2 = change in y for a 1-unit increase in x_2 when x_1 is constant

The graph of the first-order model is shown in Figure 5.3. This graph with two independent quantitative variables x_1 and x_2 plots a plane in a three-dimensional space. The plane plots the value of y for every combination (x_1, x_2). This corresponds to the points in the (x_1, x_2) plane.

Note: The terms independent, or explanatory variables, and the predictors have the same meaning and are used interchangeably in this chapter. The dependent variable is often referred to as the response variable in multiple regression.

The first-order model with two quantitative variables x_1 and x_2 is based on the assumption that there is **no interaction** between x_1 and x_2. This means that the effect on the response y of a change in x_1 (for a fixed value of x_2) is same regardless of the value of x_2 and the effect on y of a change in x_2 (for a fixed value of x_1) is same regardless of the value of x_1.

In case of simple regression analysis in the previous chapter, we presented both the manual calculations and the computer analysis of the problem. Most of the concepts we discussed for simple regression also apply to the multiple regression; however, the computations for multiple regression are more involved and require the use of matrix algebra and other mathematical concepts that are beyond the scope of this

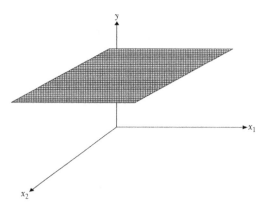

Figure 5.3 A multiple regression model with two quantitative variables

text. Therefore, in this chapter, we have provided computer analysis of the multiple linear regression models using Excel and MINITAB. The instructions to run the multiple regression using these packages are provided in the appendix (*Appendix A: Tables A.10 and A.13*). This chapter contains numerous examples with computer instructions and analysis of the computer results. The assumptions and the interpretation of the multiple linear regression models are similar to that of the simple linear regression. As we provide the analysis, we will point out the similarities and the differences between the simple and multiple regression models.

Assumptions of Multiple Regression Model

As discussed earlier, the relationship between the response variable (y) to the independent variables x_1, x_2, ..., x_k in the multiple regression is assumed to be a model of the form $y = \beta_0 + \beta_1 x_1 + \beta_2 x_2 + \beta_3 x_3 + ... + \beta_k x_k + \varepsilon$ where $\beta_0, \beta_1, \beta_2, ..., \beta_k$ are the regression coefficients, and ε is the associated error term. The multiple regression model is based on the following assumptions about the error term ε.

1. The **independence of errors** assumption. The assumption—**independence of errors** means that the errors are independent of each other. That is, the error for a set of values of independent variables is not related to the error for any other set of values of independent variables. This assumption is critical when the data are collected over different time periods. When the data are collected over time, the errors in one time period may be correlated with another time period.

2. The **normality assumption**. This means that the errors or residuals (ε_i) calculated using ($y_i - \hat{y}$) are normally distributed. The normality assumption in regression is fairly robust against departures from normality. Unless the distribution of errors is extremely different from normal, the inferences about the regression parameters $\beta_0, \beta_1, \beta_2, ..., \beta_k$ are not affected seriously.

3. The **error assumption**. The error, ε is a random variable with mean or expected value of zero, that is, $E(\varepsilon) = 0$. This implies that the mean values of the dependent variable y, for a given value of the

independent variable, x is the expected, or the mean value of y denoted by $E(y)$ and the population regression model can be written as: $E(y) = \beta_0 + \beta_1 x_1 + \beta_2 x_2 + \beta_3 x_3 + \ldots + \beta_k x_k$.

4. **Equality of variance assumption.** This assumption requires that the variance of the errors (ε_i), denoted by σ^2 are constant for all values of the independent variables x_1, x_2, ..., x_k. In case of serious departure from the equality of variance assumption, methods such as weighted least-squares, or data transformation may be used.

Note: The terms error and residual have the same meaning and these terms are used interchangeably in this chapter.

Computer Analysis of Multiple Regression

In this section, we provide a computer analysis of multiple regression. Owing to the complexity involved in the computation, computer software is always used to model and solve regression problems. We discuss the steps using MINITAB and Excel.

Problem description: The home heating cost is believed to be related to the average outside temperature, size of the house, and the age of the heating furnace. A multiple regression model is to be fitted to investigate the relationship between the heating cost and the three predictors or independent variables. The data in Table 5.1 show the average temperature (x_1), house size (x_2) in thousands of square feet, the age of the furnace (x_3) in years, and the home heating cost (y). The home heating cost is the response variable and the other three variables are predictors. The data for this problem are available in MINITAB data file: **HEAT_COST.MTW**, Excel data file: **HEAT_COST.xlsx** and is also listed later.

(a) Constructing Scatterplots and Matrix Plots

We begin our analysis by constructing scatterplots and matrix plots of the data. These plots provide useful information about the model.

We first construct scatterplots of the response (y) versus each of the independent or predictor variables. If the scatterplots of y on the

Table 5.1 *Data for home heating cost*

Row	Avg. temp.	House size	Age of furnace	Heating cost
1	37	3.0	6	210
2	30	4.0	9	365
3	37	2.5	4	182
4	61	1.0	3	65
5	66	2.0	5	82
6	39	3.5	4	205
7	15	4.1	6	360
8	8	3.8	9	295
9	22	2.9	10	235
10	56	2.2	4	125
11	55	2.0	3	78
12	40	3.8	4	162
13	21	4.5	12	405
14	40	5.0	6	325
15	61	1.8	5	82
16	21	4.2	7	277
17	63	2.3	2	99
18	41	3.0	10	195
19	28	4.2	7	240
20	31	3.0	4	144
21	33	3.2	4	265
22	31	4.2	11	355
23	36	2.8	3	175
24	56	1.2	4	57
25	35	2.3	8	196
26	36	3.6	6	215
27	9	4.3	8	380
28	10	4.0	11	300
29	21	3.0	9	240
30	51	2.5	7	130

independent variables appear to be linear enough, a multiple regression model can be fitted. Based on the analysis of the scatterplots of y and each of the independent variables, an appropriate model (e.g., a first-order model) can be recommended to predict the home heating cost.

A first-order multiple regression model does not include any higher order terms (e.g., x^2). *An example of a first-order model with five independent variables can be written as:*

$$y = b_0 + b_1 x_1 + b_2 x_2 + b_3 x_3 + b_4 x_4 + b_5 x_5 \qquad (5.6)$$

The multiple linear regression model is based on the assumption that the relationship between the response and the independent variables is linear. This relationship can be checked using a *matrix plot*. The matrix plot is used to investigate the relationships between pairs of variables by creating an array of scatterplots. MINITAB provides two options for constructing the matrix plot: *matrix of plots* and *each Y versus each X*. The first of these plots is used to investigate the relationships among pairs of variables when there are several independent variables involved. The other plot (each *y* versus each *x*) produces separate plots of the response *y* and each of the explanatory or independent variable. The instructions for constructing these scatterplots using MINITAB are provided in *Appendix A_Table A.11*.

Recall that in a simple regression, a scatterplot was constructed to investigate the relationship between the response *y* and the predictor *x*. A matrix plot should be constructed when two or more independent variables are investigated. To investigate the relationships between the response and each of the independent or explanatory variables before fitting a multiple regression model, a matrix plot may prove to be very useful. The plot allows graphically visualizing the possible relationship between response and independent variables. The plot is also very helpful in investigating and verifying the linearity assumption of multiple regression and to determine which explanatory variables are good predictors of *y*. For this example, we have constructed matrix plots using different options in MINITAB.

Figure 5.4 shows such a matrix plot (each *y* versus each *x*). In this plot, the response variable *y* is plotted with each of the independent variables. The plot shows scatterplots for heating cost (*y*) versus each of the independent variables: average temperature, house size, and age of the furnace. An investigation of the plot shows an inverse relationship between the heating cost and the average temperature (the heating cost decreases as the temperature rises) and a positive relationship between the heating cost and each of the other two variables: house size and age of the furnace. The heating cost increases with the increasing house size and also with the older furnace. None of these plots show bending (nonlinear or curvilinear) patterns between the response and the explanatory variables. The presence of bending patterns in these plots would suggest

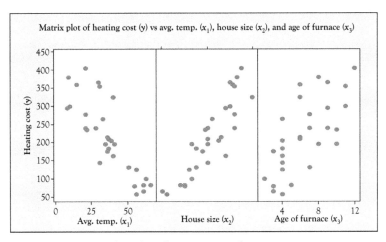

Figure 5.4 Matrix plot of each y versus each x

transformation of variables. The scatterplots in Figure 5.4 (also known as *side-by-side scatterplots*) show linear relationship between the response and each of the explanatory variables indicating all the three explanatory variables could be a good predictor of the home heating cost. In this case, a multiple linear regression would be an adequate model for predicting the heating cost.

(b) Matrix of Plots: Simple

Another variation of the matrix plot is known as "matrix of plots" in MINITAB and is shown in Figure 5.5. The computer instructions are in *Appendix A_Table A.12*. This plot provides scatterplots that are helpful in visualizing not only the relationship of the response variable with each of the independent variables but also provides scatterplots that are useful in assessing the interaction effects between the variables. This plot can be used when more detailed model beyond a first-order model is of interest. Note that the first-order model is the one that contains only the first-order terms; with no square or interaction terms and is written as $y = b_0 + b_1 x_1 + b_2 x_2 + \ldots + b_k x_k$.

The matrix plot in Figure 5.5 is a table of scatterplots with each cell showing a scatterplot of the variable that is labeled for the column versus the variable labeled for the row. The cell in the first row and first column

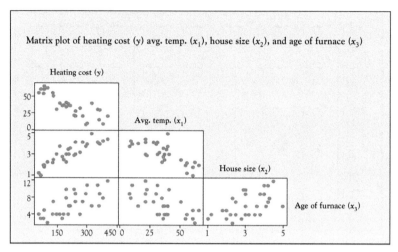

Figure 5.5 Matrix plot

displays the scatterplot of heating cost (y) versus average temperature (x_1). The plot in the second row and first column is the scatterplot of heating cost (y) and the house size (x_2) and the plot in the third row and the first column shows the scatterplot of heating cost (y) and the age of the furnace (x_3).

The second column and the second row of the matrix plot shows a scatterplot displaying the relationship between average temperature (x_1) and the house size (x_2). The scatterplots showing the relationship between the pairs of independent variables are obtained from columns two and three of the matrix plot. The matrix plot is helpful in visualizing the interaction relationships. For fitting the first-order model, a plot of y versus each x is adequate.

The matrix plots in Figures 5.4 and 5.5 show a negative association or relationship between the heating cost (y) and the average temperature (x_1) and a positive association or relationship between the heating cost (y) and the other two explanatory variables: house size (x_2) and the age of the furnace (x_3). All these relationships are linear indicating that all the three explanatory variables can be used to build a multiple regression model. Constructing the matrix plot and investigating the relationships between the variables can be very helpful in building a correct regression model.

(c) Multiple Linear Regression Model

Since a first-order model can be used adequately to predict the home heating cost, we will fit a multiple linear regression model of the form

$$y = b_0 + b_1 x_1 + b_2 x_2 + b_3 x_3$$

where y = Home heating cost (in \$)

$\quad x_1$ = Average temperature (in °F)

$\quad x_2$ = Size of the house (in thousands of square feet)

$\quad x_3$ = Age of the furnace (in years)

Table 5.1 and data file **HEAT_COST.MTW** show the data for this problem. We used MINITAB to run the regression model for this problem. The instructions for running the multiple regression using Excel are in *Appendix A _Table A.10*. MINITAB instructions are in *Appendix A_ Table A.13*.

Table 5.2 shows the result of running the multiple regression using MINITAB. In this table, we have marked some of the calculations (e.g., b_0, b_1, s_{b_0}, s_{b_1}, etc. for clarity and explanation). These are not the part of the computer output. The regression computer output has two parts: **Regression Analysis** and **Analysis of Variance** (ANOVA).

Table 5.2 MINITAB regression analysis results

```
Regression analysis: Heating cost versus Avg. temp., house size, ...

The regression equation is

Heating cost = 44.4 − 1.65 Avg. temp. + 57.5 House size + 7.91 Age of furnace

                                              Regression coefficients

Predictor        Coef          SE Coef        T        P
Constant         44.39  (b₀)   59.07  (s_b0)  0.75     0.459
Avg. temp.      -1.6457 (b₁)   0.6967 (s_b1) -2.36     0.026
House size       57.46  (b₂)   10.35  (s_b2)  5.55     0.000
Age of furnace   7.908  (b₃)   3.294  (s_b3)  2.40     0.024


S = 37.3174    R-Sq = 88.0%   R-Sq(adj) = 86.6%


Analysis of Variance                  SSE

Source          DF      SS      MS       F        P
Regression       3   2,65,777  88,592   63.62   0.000
Residual error  26    36,207   1,393
Total           29   301,985
```

(d) The Regression Equation

Refer to the "Regression Analysis" part of Table 5.2 for analysis. Since there are three independent or explanatory variables, the regression equation is of the form:

$$y = b_0 + b_1 x_1 + b_2 x_2 + b_3 x_3$$

The regression equation from the computer output is

Heating cost = 44.4 − 1.65 Avg. temp. + 57.5 House size
+ 7.91 Age of furnace   (5.7)

or

$$\hat{y} = 44.4 - 1.65 x_1 + 57.5 x_2 + 7.91 x_3 \qquad (5.8)$$

where y is the response variable (heating cost), x_1, x_2, x_3 are the independent variables as described earlier, the regression coefficients b_0, b_1, b_2, b_3 are stored under the column **Coef.** In the regression equation, these coefficients appear in rounded form.

The regression equation that can be stated in the form of Equation 5.7 or 5.8 is the estimated regression equation relating the heating cost to all the three independent variables.

(e) Interpreting the Regression Equation

Equation 5.7 or 5.8 can be interpreted in the following way:

- $b_1 = -1.65$ means that for each unit increase in the average temperature (x_1), the heating cost y (in \$) can be predicted to go down by 1.65 (or \$1.65) when the house size (x_2) and the age of the furnace (x_3) are held constant.
- $b_2 = +57.5$ means that for each unit increase in the house size (x_2 in thousands of square feet), the heating cost y (in \$) can be predicted to go up by 57.5 when the average temperature (x_1) and the age of the furnace (x_3) are held constant.

- $b_3 = 7.91$ means that for each unit increase in the age of the furnace (x_3 in years), the heating cost y can be predicted to go up by \$7.91 when the average temperature (x_1) and the house size (x_2) are held constant.

(f) Standard Error of the Estimate (s) and Its Meaning

The standard error of the estimate or the standard deviation of the model s is a measure of scatter or the measure of variation of the points around the regression hyperplane. A small value of s is desirable for a good regression model. The estimation of y is more accurate for smaller values of s. The value of the standard error of estimate is reported in the Regression Analysis (see Table 5.2). This value is measured in terms of the response variable (y). For our example, the standard error of the estimate,

$$s = \$37.32$$

The standard error of the estimate is used to check the utility of the model and to provide a measure of reliability of the prediction made from the model. One interpretation of s is that the interval $\pm 2s$ will provide an approximation to the accuracy with which the regression model will predict the future value of the response y for given values of x. Thus, for our example, we can expect the model to provide predictions of heating cost (y) to be within $\pm 2s = \pm 2(37.32) = \pm\$74.64$.

(g) The Coefficient of Multiple Determination (r^2)

The coefficient of multiple determination is often used to check the adequacy of the regression model. The value of r^2 lies between 0 and 1, or 0% and 100%, that is, $0 \le r^2 \le 1$. It indicates the fraction of total variation of the dependent variable y that is explained by the independent variables or predictors. Usually, closer the value of r^2 to 1 or 100%, the stronger is the model. However, one should be careful in drawing conclusions based solely on the value of r^2. A large value of r^2 does not necessarily mean that the model provides a good fit to the data. In case of multiple regression, addition of a new variable to the model always increases the value of r^2

even if the added variable is not statistically significant. Thus, addition of a new variable will increase r^2 indicating a stronger model but may lead to poor predictions of new values. The value of r^2 can be calculated using the expression:

$$r^2 = 1 - \frac{SSE}{SST} \quad \text{or} \qquad (5.9)$$

$$r^2 = \frac{SSR}{SST} \qquad (5.10)$$

In these equations, SSE is the sum of square of errors (unexplained variation or error), SST is the total sum of squares, and SSR is the sum of squares due to regression (explained variation). These values can be read from the "*Analysis of Variance*" part of Table 5.2. From this table:

$$r^2 = 1 - \frac{SSE}{SST} = 1 - \frac{36207}{301985} = 0.88$$

$$r^2 = \frac{SSR}{SST} = \frac{265777}{301985} = 0.88$$

The value of r^2 is calculated and reported in the "Regression Analysis" part of Table 5.2. For our example the coefficient of multiple determination r^2 (reported as **R-sq**) is:

$$r^2 = 88.0\%$$

This means that 88.0% of the variability in y is explained by the three independent variables used in the model. Note that $r^2 = 0$ implies a complete lack of fit of the model to the data, whereas $r^2 = 1$ implies a perfect fit.

The value of $r^2 = 88.0\%$ for our example implies that using the three independent variables: average temperature, size of the house, and the age of the furnace in the model, 88.0% of the total variation in heating cost (y) can be explained. The statistic r^2 tells how well the model fits the data, and thus, provides the overall predictive usefulness of the model.

(h) The Adjusted r^2

The adjusted r^2 is the coefficient of multiple determination adjusted for the independent or predictor variables and the sample size. This value is calculated using the following expression:

$$r^2 - adj = 1 - \left[(1 - r^2) \frac{(n-1)}{n - (k+1)} \right] \qquad (5.11)$$

where r^2 is the coefficient of multiple determination, n is the number of observations or the sample size, and k is the number of independent variables in the model. For our example, $r^2 = 88\%$ (from Table 5.2), $n = 30$, and $k = 3$. Substituting these values in Equation 5.11:

$$r^2 - adj = 1 - \left[(1 - r^2) \frac{(n-1)}{n - (k+1)} \right] = 1 - \left[(1 - 0.88) \frac{(30-1)}{30 - (3+1)} \right] = 0.866$$

This value is reported as:

$$R\text{-}Sq(\text{adj.}) = 86.6\%$$

in the "*Regression Analysis*" part of Table 5.2.

The values of r^2 and r^2-adjusted have similar interpretation but unlike r^2, r^2-adjusted takes into account or "adjusts" for the sample size n and the number of β parameters in the model. The value of r^2-adjusted is always less than r^2 and cannot be forced to become 1 by adding more and more predictors or independent variables to the model. Therefore, r^2-adjusted is often preferred in choosing a measure of the model adequacy. However, r^2 and r^2-adjusted are only sample statistic; therefore, the model adequacy should not be judged based solely on these values. A better method of judging the overall usefulness or the significance of the regression model is to conduct a test of hypothesis involving all the β parameters (except β_0). This hypothesis test is explained in the next section.

The value of adjusted r^2 is also used in comparing two regression models that have the same response variable but different number of independent variables or predictors. The adjusted r^2 value of 86.6% means that 86.6% of the variability in heating cost y can be explained by this model, which is adjusted for the number of independent variables k and the sample size n.

Hypothesis Tests in Multiple Regression

In multiple regression, two types of hypothesis tests are conducted to measure the model adequacy. These are:

1. Hypothesis test for the overall usefulness, or significance of regression; and
2. Hypothesis tests on the individual regression coefficients.

The test for overall significance of regression can be conducted using the information in the "*Analysis of Variance*" part of Table 5.2. The information contained in the "*Regression Analysis*" part of this table is used to conduct the tests on the individual regression coefficients using the "T" or "p" column. These tests are explained in the following.

Testing the Overall Significance of Regression

Recall that in simple regression analysis, we conducted the test for the significance using a *t-test* and *F-test*. Both these tests in simple regression provided the same conclusion. If the null hypothesis was rejected in these tests, it led to the conclusion that the slope was not zero, or $\beta_1 = 0$. In a multiple regression, the *t-test* and the *F-test* have somewhat different interpretations. These tests have the following objectives:

1. The F-test in a multiple regression is used to test the overall significance of the regression. This test is conducted to determine whether a significant relationship exists between the response variable y and the set of independent variables, or predictors $x_1, x_2, ..., x_n$.
2. If the conclusion of the F-test indicates that the regression is significant overall, then a separate *t-test* is conducted for each of the

independent variables to determine whether each of the independent variables is significant.

Both the *F*-test and *t*-test are explained in the following.

F-Test

The null and alternate hypotheses for the multiple regression model $y = b_0 + b_1 x_1 + b_2 x_2 + \ldots + b_k x_k$ are stated as:

$$H_0 : \beta_1 = \beta_2 = \ldots = \beta_k = 0 \text{ (regression is not significant)}$$

$$H_1 : \text{at least one of the coefficients is nonzero} \qquad (5.12)$$

If the null hypothesis H_0 is rejected, we conclude that at least one of the independent variables $x_1, x_2, \ldots, x_n$ contributes significantly to the prediction of the response variable y. If H_0 is not rejected, then none of the independent variables contributes to the prediction of y. The test statistic for testing this hypothesis uses an *F*-statistic and is given by:

$$F = \frac{\text{MSR}}{\text{MSE}} \qquad (5.13)$$

where MSR = mean squares due to regression, or *explained* variability, and MSE = mean square error, or unexplained variability. In Equation 5.13, the larger the explained variation of the total variability, the larger is the *F*-statistic. The values of MSR, MSE, and the *F*-statistic are calculated in the "*Analysis of Variance*" *table* of the multiple regression computer output (see Table 5.3).

The critical value for the test is given by $F_{k, n-(k+1), \alpha}$ where, k is the number of independent variables, n is the number of observations in the model, and α is the level of significance. Note that k and $(n - k - 1)$ are the degrees of freedom (DF) associated with MSR and MSE, respectively. The null hypothesis is rejected if $F > F_{k, n-(k+1), \alpha}$ where F is the calculated *F*-value or the test statistic value in the *Analysis of Variance* table.

Test the Overall Significance of Regression for the Example Problem at a 5% Level of Significance

Step 1: State the null and alternate hypotheses

For the overall significance of regression, the null and alternate hypotheses are:

$$H_0 : \beta_1 = \beta_2 = \ldots = \beta_k = 0 \text{ (regression is not significant)}$$

$$H_1 : \text{at least one of the coefficients is nonzero} \tag{5.14}$$

Step 2: Specify the test statistic to test the hypothesis

The test statistics is given by:

$$F = \frac{\text{MSR}}{\text{MSE}} \tag{5.15}$$

The value of F-statistic is obtained from the "*Analysis of Variance*" (ANOVA) table of the computer output. We have reproduced the *Analysis of Variance* part of the following table. In this table, the labels k, $[n - (k + 1)]$, SSR, SSE, and so on are added for explanation purpose. They are not part of the computer results.

In this ANOVA table, the first column refers to the sources of variation, DF = the degrees of freedom, SS = the sum of squares, MS = mean squares, F = the F-statistic, and p is the probability or p-value associated with the calculated F-statistic.

The DF for Regression and Error are k and $n - (k + 1)$, respectively, where k is the number of independent variables ($k = 3$ for our example) and n is the number of observations ($n = 30$). Also, the total sum of

Table 5.3 Analysis of variance table

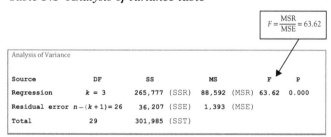

Analysis of Variance					
Source	DF	SS	MS	F	P
Regression	k = 3	265,777 (SSR)	88,592 (MSR)	63.62	0.000
Residual error	n − (k + 1) = 26	36,207 (SSE)	1,393 (MSE)		
Total	29	301,985 (SST)			

$$F = \frac{\text{MSR}}{\text{MSE}} = 63.62$$

squares (SST) is partitioned into two parts: sum of squares due to regression (SSR) and the sum of squares due to error (SSE) having the following relationship:

$$SST = SSR + SSE$$

We have labeled SST, SSR, and SSE values in Table 5.3. The mean square due to regression (MSR) and the mean squares due to error (MSE) are calculated using the following relationships:

$$MSR = SSR/k \text{ and } MSE = SSE/(n - k - 1)$$

The F-test statistic is calculated as $F = MSR/MSE$.

Step 3: Determine the value of the test statistic

The test statistic value or the F-statistic from the ANOVA table (see Table 5.3) is:

$$F = 63.62$$

Step 4: Specify the critical value

The critical value is given by:

$$F_{k,n-(k+1),\alpha} = F_{3,26,0.05} = 2.74 \text{ (from the } F\text{-table)}$$

Figure 5.6 shows the rejection and nonrejection region for this test.

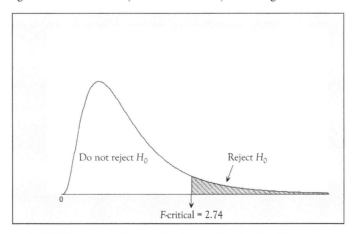

Figure 5.6 Rejection and nonrejection region for the F-test

Step 5: Specify the decision rule

Reject H_0 if F-statistic > $F_{critical}$

Step 6: Reach a decision and state your conclusion

The calculated F-statistic value is 63.62. Since $F = 63.62 > F_{critical} = 2.74$, we reject the null hypothesis stated in Equation 5.14 and conclude that the regression is significant overall. This indicates that there exists a significant relationship between the dependent and independent variables.

Alternate Method of Testing the Preceding Hypothesis

The hypothesis stated using Equation 5.14 can also be tested using the p-value approach. The decision rule using the p-value approach is given by:

$$\text{If } p \geq \alpha, \text{ do not reject } H_0$$

$$\text{If } p < \alpha, \text{ reject } H_0$$

From Table 5.3, the calculated p-value is 0.000 (see the P column). Since $p = 0.000 < \alpha = 0.05$, we reject the null hypothesis H_0 and conclude that the regression is significant overall.

Hypothesis Tests on Individual Regression Coefficients

t-tests

If the F-test shows that the regression is significant, a *t-test* on individual regression coefficients is conducted to determine whether a particular independent variable is significant. We are often interested in determining which of the independent variables contributes to the prediction of y. The hypothesis test described here can be used for this purpose.

To determine which of the independent variables contributes to the prediction of the dependent variable y, the following hypotheses test can be conducted:

$$H_0 : \beta_j = 0$$
$$H_1 : \beta_j \neq 0$$

(5.16)

This hypothesis tests an individual regression coefficient. If the null hypothesis H_0 is rejected, it indicates that the independent variable x_j is significant and contributes in the prediction of y. On the other hand, if the null hypothesis H_0 is not rejected, then x_j is not a significant variable and can be deleted from the model or further investigated. The test is repeated for each of the independent variables in the model.

This hypothesis test also helps to determine if the model can be made more effective by deleting certain independent variables, or by adding extra variables. The information to conduct the hypothesis test for each of the independent variables is contained in the *"Regression Analysis"* part of the computer output, which is reproduced in Table 5.4. The columns labeled T and P are used to test the hypotheses. Since there are three independent variables, we will test to determine whether each of the three variables is a significant variable; that is, if each of the independent variables contributes in the prediction of y. The hypothesis to be tested and the test procedure are explained in the following. We will use a significance level of $\alpha = 0.05$ for testing each of the independent variables.

Test the hypothesis that each of the three independent variables is significant at a 5% level of significance.

Table 5.4 MINITAB regression analysis results

```
Regression analysis: Heating cost versus Avg. temp., House size, ...

The regression equation is

Heating cost = 44.4 - 1.65 Avg. temp. + 57.5 House size + 7.91 Age of
furnace
```

Predictor	Coef	SE Coef	T	P
Constant	44.39 (b_0)	59.07 (s_{b0})	0.75	0.459
Avg. temp.	−1.6457 (b_1)	0.6967 (s_{b1})	−2.36	0.026
House size	57.46 (b_2)	10.35 (s_{b2})	5.55	0.000
Age of furnace	7.908 (b_3)	3.294 (s_{b3})	2.40	0.024

$S = 37.3174$ $R\text{-}Sq = 88.0\%$ $R\text{-}Sq(\text{adj}) = 86.6\%$

$$t = \frac{b_1}{s_{b_1}} = \frac{-1.6457}{0.6967} = -2.36$$

Analysis of Variance

Source	DF	SS	MS	F	P
Regression	3	265,777	88,592	63.62	0.000
Residual error	26	36,207	1,393		
Total	29	301,985			

Test for the significance of x_1 or Average Temperature

Step 1: State the null and alternate hypotheses

The null and alternate hypotheses are:

$$H_0 : \beta_1 = 0 \; (x_1 \text{ is not significant or } x_1 \text{ does not contribute in prediction of } y)$$

$$H_1 : \beta_1 \neq 0 \; (x_1 \text{ is significant or } x_1 \text{ does contribute in prediction of } y) \qquad (5.17)$$

Step 2: Specify the test statistic to test the hypothesis

The test statistics is given by:

$$t = \frac{b_1}{s_{b_1}} \qquad (5.18)$$

where b_1 is the estimate of slope β_1 and s_{b_1} is the estimated standard deviation of b_1.

Step 3: Determine the value of the test statistic

The values b_1, s_{b_1}, and t are all reported in the *Regression Analysis* part of Table 5.4. From this table, the value for the variable x_1 or the average temperature (avg. temp.) is:

$$b_1 = -1.6457, \; s_{b_1} = 0.6967$$

and the test statistic value is:

$$t = \frac{b_1}{s_{b_1}} = \frac{-1.6457}{0.6967} = -2.36$$

This value is reported under the T column.

Step 4: Specify the critical value

The **critical values** for the test are given by:

$$t_{\alpha/2, [n-(k+1)]}$$

which is the t-value from the t-table for $[n - (k + 1)]$ DF and $\alpha/2$, where n is the number of observations ($n = 30$), k is the number of independent variables ($k = 3$), and α is the level of significance (0.05 in this case). Thus,

$$t_{\alpha/2,[n-(k+1)]} = t_{0.025,[30-(3+1)]} = t_{0.025,26} = 2.056 \ \ (\text{from the } t\text{-table})$$

The areas of rejection and nonrejection are shown in Figure 5.7.

Step 5: Specify the decision rule—The decision rule for the test:

$$\text{Reject } H_0 \text{ if } t > +2.056$$

$$\text{or if } t < -2.056$$

Step 6: Reach a decision and state your conclusion
The test statistic value (t-value) for the variable "*avg. temp.*" (x_1) from Table 5.4 is –2.36.

$$\text{Since, } t = -2.36 < t_{\text{critical}} = -2.056$$

We reject the null hypothesis H_0 (stated in Equation 5.17) and conclude that the variable average temperature (x_1) is a significant variable and does contribute in the prediction of y.

The significance of other independent variables can be tested in the same way. The test statistic or the t-values for all the independent variables

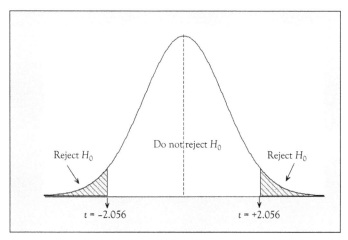

Figure 5.7 Areas of rejection and nonrejection for the t-test

are reported in Table 5.4 under T column. The critical values for testing each independent variable are the same as in the test for the first independent variable shown earlier. Thus, the critical values for testing the other independent variables are:

$$t_{\alpha/2,[n-(k+1)]} = t_{0.025,[30-(3+1)]} = t_{0.025,26} = \pm 2.056$$

The areas of rejection and nonrejection are the same as in Figure 5.7.

Alternate Way of Testing the Previous Hypothesis

The hypothesis stated using Equation 5.17 can also be tested using the p-value approach. The decision rule for the p-value approach is given by:

$$\text{If } p \geq \alpha, \text{ do not reject } H_0$$

$$\text{If } p < \alpha, \text{ reject } H_0 \qquad (5.19)$$

From Table 5.4, the p-value for the variable average temperature (avg. temp. x_1) is 0.026. Since, $p = 0.026 < \alpha = 0.05$, we reject H_0 and conclude that the variable average temperature (x_1) is a significant variable.

(i) Test for the other independent variables

The other two independent variables are

x_2 = Size of the house (or House Size)
x_3 = Age of the furnace

It is usually more convenient to test the hypothesis using the p-value approach. Table 5.5 provides a summary of the tests using the p-value approach for all the three independent variables. The significance level α is 0.05 for all the tests. The hypothesis can be stated as:

$$H_0: \beta_j = 0 \ (x_j \text{ is not a significant variable})$$

$$H_1: \beta_j \neq 0 \ (x_j \text{ is a significant variable})$$

where j = 1, 2, ... 3 for our example.

Table 5.5 Summary table

Independent variable	p-value from Table 5.4	Compare p to α	Decision	Significant? Yes or no
Av. temp. (x_1)	0.026	$p < \alpha$	Reject H_0	Yes
House size (x_2)	0.000	$p < \alpha$	Reject H_0	Yes
Age furnace (x_3)	0.024	$p < \alpha$	Reject H_0	Yes

From Table 5.5, it can be seen that all the independent variables are significant. This means that all the three independent variables contribute in predicting the response variable y, the heating cost.

Note: The preceding method of conducting t-tests on each β parameter in a model is not the best way to determine whether the overall model is providing information for the prediction of y. In this method, we need to conduct a t-test for each independent variable to determine whether the variable is significant. Conducting a series of t-tests increases the likelihood of making an error in deciding which variable to retain in the model and which one to exclude. For example, suppose we are fitting a first-order model like the one in this example with 10 independent variables and decided to conduct t-tests on all 10 of the βs. Suppose each test is conducted at $\alpha = 0.05$. This means that there is a 5% chance of making a wrong or incorrect decision (type I error—probability of rejecting a true null hypothesis) and there is a 95% chance of making a right decision. If 10 tests are conducted, the probability of making a correct decision drops to approximately 60% $[(0.95)^{10} = 0.599]$ assuming that all the tests are independent of each other. This means that even if all the β parameters (except β_0) are equal to 0, approximately 40% of the time, the null hypothesis will be rejected incorrectly at least once leading to the conclusion that β differs from 0. Thus, in the multiple regression models where a large number of independent variables are involved and a series of t-tests are conducted, there is a chance of including a large number of insignificant variables and excluding some useful ones from the model. In order to assess the utility of the multiple regression models, we need to conduct a test that will include all the β parameters simultaneously. Such a test would test the overall significance of the multiple regression model. The other useful measure of the utility of the model would be to find some statistical quantity such as r^2 that measures how well the model fits the data.

A Note on Checking the Utility of a Multiple Regression Model (Checking the Model Adequacy)

Step 1. To test the overall adequacy of a regression model, first test the following null and alternate hypotheses:

$$H_0 : \beta_1 = \beta_2 = \ldots = \beta_k = 0 \text{ (no relationship)}$$

$$H_1 : \text{at least one of the coefficients is nonzero}$$

(a) If the null hypothesis is rejected, there is evidence that all the β parameters are not zero and the model is adequate. Go to Step 2.

(b) If the null hypothesis is not rejected then the overall regression model is not adequate. In this case, fit another model with more independent variables, or consider higher order terms.

Step 2. If the overall model is adequate, conduct t-tests on the β parameters of interest, or the parameters considered to be most important in the model. Avoid conducting a series of t-tests on the β parameters. It will increase the probability of type I error α.

Inferences about the β Parameters

For the heating cost example, we would expect that the heating cost will decrease linearly as the average temperature (x_1) increases. To confirm this, suppose we hypothesize that the heating cost (y) will decrease linearly as the average temperature (x_1) increases. Use the information in the MINITAB regression printout in Table 5.4 to test the hypothesis that the mean home heating cost decreases as the average temperature increases when the size of the house (x_2) and age of the furnace (x_3) are held constant, that is, $\beta_1 < 0$. Use $\alpha = 0.05$. In this case, we would like to test the following hypotheses:

$$H_0 : \beta_1 = 0$$

$$H_1 : \beta_1 < 0$$

(5.20)

The test statistic for testing this hypothesis:

$$t = \frac{b_1}{s_{b_1}}$$
(5.21)

The values of b_1, s_{b_1}, and t are reported under the "*Regression Analysis*" (Table 5.4). From this table, these values for the variable x_1 or the average temperature (avg. temp.) are:

$$b_1 = -1.6457, \; s_{b_1} = 0.6967$$

and the test statistic value:

$$t = \frac{b_1}{s_{b_1}} = \frac{-1.6457}{0.6967} = -2.36$$
(5.22)

The **critical value** for the test is given by:

$$t_{\alpha, n-(k+1)}$$

which is the t-value from the t-table for $[n - (k + 1)]$ DF and α, where n is the number of observations ($n = 30$), k is the number of independent variables ($k = 3$), and α is the level of significance (0.05 in this case). Thus,

$$t_{\alpha,[n-(k+1)]} = t_{0.05,[30-(3+1)]} = t_{0.05,26} = 1.706 \;\; \text{(from the t-table)}$$

The areas of rejection and nonrejection are shown in Figure 5.8.

The test statistic value $t = -2.36$ given by Equation 5.22 falls in the rejection region; therefore, we have sufficient evidence to reject H_0 and conclude that the heating cost (y) decreases as the average temperature increases.

Confidence and Prediction Intervals

The confidence and prediction intervals for the multiple regression model can be calculated using a computer package. The steps to calculate these intervals using MINITAB are similar to that of simple regression.

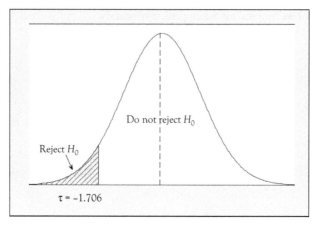

Figure 5.8 Rejection region for $H_0: \beta_1 = 0$ versus $H_0: \beta_1 < 0$

Table 5.6 shows these calculated intervals for our example problem (the original data is in Table 5.1 also provided in data file **HEAT_COST**). The intervals are calculated for the given values of the independent variables x_1, x_2, and x_3. Here we provide a discussion on these intervals. In Table 5.6, the **Fits** are the fitted values or $\hat{y}$, and the **SEs of fits** are the standard error of the fits.

Interpreting Confidence Intervals and Prediction Intervals for an Individual Observation in Table 5.6

The interpretation of the confidence intervals on the mean response at the given values of the independent variables x_1, x_2, x_3 and also the prediction intervals at these given values of the independent variables are discussed here.

The "Fits" ($\hat{y}$) are calculated using the fitted regression equation. The regression equation for our example is:

Heating cost = 44.4 − 1.65 Avg. temp. + 57.5 House size + 7.91 Age of furnace or,

$$\hat{y} = 44.4 - 1.65x_1 + 57.5x_2 + 7.91x_3 \qquad (5.23)$$

Table 5.6 Confidence and prediction intervals

New Obs	Fit	SE Fit	95% CI	95% PI
1	203.33	6.95	(189.05, 217.61)	(125.31, 281.36)
2	296.04	11.03	(273.37, 318.71)	(216.05, 376.03)
3	158.79	11.45	(135.25, 182.33)	(78.55, 239.02)
4	25.19	16.14	(-7.99, 58.37)	(-58.39, 108.77)
5	90.24	15.48	(58.43, 122.05)	(7.20, 173.28)
6	212.96	11.33	(189.66, 236.25)	(132.79, 293.12)
7	302.75	14.29	(273.36, 332.13)	(220.60, 384.89)
8	320.75	15.08	(289.75, 351.75)	(238.02, 403.48)
9	253.90	15.06	(222.95, 284.85)	(171.19, 336.62)
10	110.28	10.70	(88.29, 132.27)	(30.48, 190.08)
11	92.53	11.48	(68.92, 116.13)	(12.27, 172.78)
12	228.55	13.37	(201.06, 256.04)	(147.07, 310.03)
13	363.30	16.88	(328.61, 398.00)	(279.12, 447.49)
14	313.32	22.19	(267.71, 358.93)	(224.08, 402.56)
15	86.98	13.35	(59.54, 114.41)	(5.51, 168.44)
16	306.53	10.82	(284.29, 328.76)	(226.66, 386.39)
17	88.69	14.62	(58.64, 118.74)	(6.31, 171.07)
18	228.38	15.31	(196.91, 259.85)	(145.47, 311.29)
19	295.01	10.58	(273.26, 316.75)	(215.28, 374.74)
20	197.39	12.32	(172.07, 222.72)	(116.61, 278.17)
21	205.59	11.32	(182.32, 228.86)	(125.43, 285.75)
22	321.70	16.62	(287.54, 355.86)	(237.73, 405.67)
23	169.76	13.25	(142.53, 196.99)	(88.36, 251.16)
24	52.82	15.07	(21.84, 83.80)	(-29.91, 135.55)
25	182.22	12.89	(155.71, 208.72)	(101.06, 263.37)
26	239.46	8.47	(222.04, 256.87)	(160.80, 318.12)
27	339.93	14.00	(311.15, 368.71)	(258.00, 421.86)
28	344.77	14.74	(314.47, 375.06)	(262.30, 427.24)
29	253.39	13.31	(226.03, 280.75)	(171.95, 334.83)
30	159.47	11.72	(135.37, 183.57)	(79.07, 239.87)

Note: 95% CI: 95% Confidence Interval 95% PI: 95% Prediction Interval.

where x_1, x_2, and x_3 are the independent variables. For the first row of the data file in Table 5.1, the values are $x_1 = 37$, $x_2 = 3.0$, and $x_3 = 6.0$. Substituting these values in the fitted regression equation, we get:

$$\hat{y} = 44.4 - 1.65(37) + 57.5(3.0) + 7.91(6) = 203.33$$

This is the predicted value of y for the given values of the independent variables aforementioned. In Table 5.6, the value is reported as the "**Fit**" in the first row and the standard error of the fit (SE Fit) is 6.95 (row 1, column 2). The confidence and prediction intervals using these values are calculated and reported as 95% CI and 95% PI.

Interpretation of Confidence and Prediction Interval

The confidence and prediction intervals in the first row of Table 5.6 (for $x_1 = 37$, $x_2 = 3.0$, and $x_3 = 6$) can be interpreted in the following ways:

- The predicted heating cost (y) is \$203.33
- The standard error of the heating cost is estimated to be \$6.95
- There is a 95% confidence that the mean heating cost is between \$189.05 and \$217.61, and
- There is a 95% chance that the heating cost for an individual home is between \$125.31 and \$281.36 (this is the prediction interval).

Note: The confidence and prediction intervals for the values of the independent variables not contained in the original data, or for other values of independent variables of interest, may also be calculated by MINITAB.

Confidence Interval for Regression Coefficients β_i

The confidence intervals for the regression coefficients can be calculated using the following expression:

$$b_i \pm t_{\alpha/2, n-(k+1)} s_{b_i} \qquad (5.24)$$

where b_i are the estimated regression coefficients; $t_{\alpha, n-(k+1)}$ is the t-value for $[n - (k + 1)]$ DF, where n is the number of observations; k is the number of independent variables in the model; and s_{b_i} are the standard deviations of the b_is. These confidence intervals are based on the assumption that the errors are normally and independently distributed with mean zero and variance σ^2.

Suppose, we wish to obtain a 95% confidence interval for the true slope β_1 [that is, the effect of the independent variable, average temperature on the heating cost (y), holding all the other independent variables constant]. The required confidence interval using Equation 5.24 can be written as:

$$b_1 \pm t_{\alpha/2,\,n-(k+1)}s_{b_1} \tag{5.25}$$

where the values of b_1 and s_{b_1} can be obtained from the computer output in Table 5.4. From this table, $b_1 = -1.6457$, $s_{b_1} = 0.6967$, and $t_{\alpha/2,\,n-(k+1)} = t_{0.025,\,30-(3+1)} = t_{0.025,\,26} = 2.056$ (from the t-table). Using these values, a 95% confidence interval for β_1 is

$$b_1 \pm t_{\alpha/2,\,n-(k+1)}s_{b_1}$$
$$-1.6457 \pm (2.056)(0.6967)$$
$$-1.6457 \pm 1.4324$$
$$-3.079 \le \beta_1 \le -0.2133$$

The previous interval means that we are 95% confident that b_1 falls between –3.08 and –0.21. Since β_1 is the slope of the line relating the heating cost (y) to the average temperature (x_1), we can conclude that the heating cost decreases between \$0.21 to \$3.08 for every one degree increase in the average temperature, holding the size of the house (x_2) and the age of the furnace (x_3) constant.

In a similar way, we can find a 95% confidence interval for the true slope β_3 or, the effect of the variable "*age of furnace,*" on the heating cost (y) holding the other predictors constant.

From Table 5.4, $b_3 = 7.908$, $s_{b_3} = 3.294$, and

$$t_{\alpha/2,\,n-(k+1)} = t_{0.025,\,30-(3+1)} = t_{0.025,\,26} = 2.056 \text{ (from the } t\text{-table).}$$

Therefore, a 95% confidence interval for β_3 is:

$$b_3 \pm t_{\alpha/2,\,n-(k+1)}s_{b_3}$$
$$7.908 \pm (2.056)(3.294)$$
$$7.908 \pm 6.772$$
$$1.136 \le \beta_3 \le 14.68$$

Thus, we are 95% confident that b_3 falls between 1.14 and 14.68. Since β_3 is the slope relating the heating cost (y) to the age of furnace (x_3), we can conclude that the heating cost increases between \$1.14 and

$14.68 for every one year increase in the age of the furnace, holding the average temperature (x_1) and the size of the house (x_2) constant.

Multicollinearity and Autocorrelation in Multiple Regression

Multicollinearity is a measure of correlation among the predictors in a regression model. Multicollinearity exists when two or more independent variables in the regression model are correlated with each other. In practice, it is not unusual to see correlations among the independent variables. However, if serious multicollinearity is present, it may cause problems by increasing the variance of the regression coefficients and making them unstable and difficult to interpret. Also, highly correlated independent variables increase the likelihood of rounding errors in the calculation of β estimates and standard errors. In the presence of multicollinearity, the regression results may be misleading.

Effects of Multicollinearity

a. Consider a regression model where the production cost (y) is related to three independent variables: machine hours (x_1), material cost (x_2), and labor hours (x_3):

$$y = \beta_0 + \beta_1 x_1 + \beta_2 x_2 + \beta_3 x_3$$

MINITAB computer output for this model is shown in Table 5.5. If we perform t-tests for testing β_1, β_2, and β_3, we find that all the three independent variables are nonsignificant at $\alpha = 0.05$ while the F-test for $H_0: \beta_1 = \beta_2 = \beta_3 = 0$ is significant (see the p-value in the *Analysis of Variance* results shown in Table 5.7). The results are contradictory but, in fact, they are not. The tests on individual b_i parameters indicate that the contribution of one variable, say $x_1 =$ machine hours is not significant after the effects of $x_2 =$ material cost, and $x_3 =$ labor hours have been accounted for. However, the result of the F-test indicates that at least one of the three variables is significant, or is making a contribution to the prediction of response y.

Table 5.7 Regression analysis: PROD COST versus MACHINE HOURS, MATERIAL COST, and LABOR Hours

```
Regression a nalysis: PROD COST versus MACHINE HOURS, MATERIAL COST,...
The regression equation is
PROD COST = -336 - 0.897 MACHINE HOURS + 0.825 MATERIAL COST
            + 0.271 LABOR HOURS

Predictor           Coef  SE Coef      T      P     VIF
Constant          -335.5    159.9  -2.10  0.044
MACHINE HOURS     -0.8973   0.8087  -1.11  0.276  24.239
MATERIAL COST      0.8247   0.4676   1.76  0.088  14.064
LABOR HOURS        0.2707   0.2276   1.19  0.243  10.846

S = 101.674   R-Sq = 45.6%   R-Sq(adj) = 40.4%

Analysis of Variance
Source          DF       SS      MS     F      P
Regression       3  269,108  89,703  8.68  0.000
Residual error  31  320,465  10,338
Total           34  589,573
```

It is also possible that at least two or all the three variables are contributing to the prediction of y. Here, the contribution of one variable is overlapping with that of the other variable or variables. This is because of the multicollinearity effect.

b. Multicollinearity may also have an effect on the signs of the parameter estimates. For example, refer to the regression equation in Table 5.7. In this model, the production cost (y) is related to the three explanatory variables: machine hours (x_1), material cost (x_2), and labor hours (x_3). If we check the effect of the variable machine hours (x_1), the regression model indicates that for each unit increase in machine hour, the production cost (y) decreases when the other two factors are held constant. However, we would expect the production cost (y) to increase as more machine hours are used. This may be due to the presence of multicollinearity. Because of the presence of multicollinearity, the value of a β parameter may have the opposite sign from what is expected.

One way of avoiding multicollinearity in regression is to conduct design of experiments and select the levels of factors in a way that the levels are uncorrelated. This may not be possible in many situations. It is not unusual to have correlated independent variables; therefore, it is important to detect the presence of multicollinearity to make the necessary modifications in the regression analysis.

Detecting Multicollinearity

Several methods are used to detect the presence of multicollinearity in regression. We will discuss two of them.

1. **Detecting multicollinearity using variance inflation factor (VIF):** MINITAB provides an option to calculate VIFs for each predictor variable that measures how much the variance of the estimated regression coefficients are inflated as compared to when the predictor variables are not linearly related. Use the guidelines in Table 5.8 to interpret the VIF.

   VIF values greater than 10 may indicate that multicollinearity is unduly influencing your regression results. In this case, you may want to reduce multicollinearity by removing unimportant independent variables from your model.

   For comparison, refer to Table 5.8 for the values of VIF for the production cost example. The VIF value for each predictor has a value greater than 10 indicating the precedence of multicollinearity. The VIF values indicate that the predictors are highly correlated. The VIF for each of the independent variables is calculated automatically when a multiple regression model is run using the MINITAB instruction in **Appendix A_Table A.13**.

2. **Detecting multicollinearity by calculating coefficient of correlation r**

   A simple way of determining multicollinearity is to calculate the coefficient of correlation r between each pair of predictor or independent variables in the model. The degree of multicollinearity

Table 5.8 Detecting correlation using VIF values

Values of VIF	Predictors are...
VIF =1	Not correlated
1 < VIF < 5	Moderately correlated
VIF = 5 to10 or greater	Highly correlated

Table 5.9 *Determining multicollinearity using correlation coefficient, r*

Correlation coefficient, r	
$|r| \geq 0.8$	Extreme multicollinearity
$0.2 \leq |r| < 0.8$	Moderate multicollinearity
$|r| < 0.2$	Low multicollinearity

Table 5.10 *Correlation coefficient between pairs of variable*

```
Correlations: MACHINE HOURS, MATERIAL COST, LABOR HOURS
                      MACHINE HOURS      MATERIAL COST (y)
MATERIAL COST          0.964
LABOR HOURS            0.953                 0.917
Cell contents: Pearson correlation
```

depends on the magnitude of the value of r. Use Table 5.9 as a guide to determine the multicollinearity.

Table 5.10 shows the correlation coefficient r between each pair of predictors for the production cost example.

The values of r in Table 5.10 show that the variables are highly correlated. The instructions to calculate the correlation coefficient matrix can be found in **Appendix A_Table A.14**.

Example 5.1

A pharmaceutical company is concerned about declining sales of one of its drugs. The drug was introduced in the market approximately two-and-a half years ago. In recent few months, the sales of this product is in constant decline and the company is concerned about losing its market share as it is one of the major drugs the company markets. The head of the sales and marketing department wants to investigate the possible causes and evaluate some strategies to boost the sales. He would like to build a regression model of the sales volume and several independent variables believed to be strongly related to the sales. A multiple regression model will help the company to determine the important variables and also predict the future sales volume. The marketing director believes that the sales volume is directly related to three major factors: dollars spent on advertisement, commission paid to the salespersons, and the number of salespersons deployed for marketing this drug. The data on these independent variables were obtained from the company records and are shown in Table 5.11. The data can also be obtained from data file: **SALES_VOLUME**. The instructions to run the multiple regression model using Excel and MINITAB can be found in **Appendix A**.

The variables in the study are: Sales volume (y) in thousands of dollars, advertisement dollars spent (x_1) in hundreds of dollars, commission paid to the salespersons (x_2) in hundreds of dollars, numbers of salespersons (x_3).

A side-by-side scatterplots of y—the sales volume and each of the independent variables: x_1—the advertisement dollars spent, x_2—the commission paid to the salespersons, and x_3—the number of salespersons is shown in Figure 5.9. The regression outputs relating y and x_1, x_2, x_3 are shown in Tables 5.12 and 5.13.

Table 5.11 Sales data for a pharmaceutical company

Row	Sales volume (y)	Advertisement (x_1)	Commission (x_2)	No. of salespersons (x_3)
1	973.62	580.17	235.48	8
2	903.12	414.67	240.78	7
3	1,067.37	420.48	276.07	10
4	1,193.37	454.59	295.70	14
5	1,429.62	524.05	286.67	16
6	1,557.87	623.77	325.66	18
7	1,590.12	641.89	298.82	17
8	1,081.62	453.03	310.19	12
9	1,088.37	495.76	242.91	13
10	1,132.62	506.73	275.88	11
11	1,314.87	490.35	337.14	15
12	1,562.37	624.24	266.30	19
13	1,050.12	459.56	240.13	10
14	1,055.37	447.03	254.18	12
15	1,112.37	493.96	237.49	14
16	1,235.37	543.84	276.70	16
17	1,518.12	618.38	271.14	18
18	1,574.37	620.50	281.94	15
19	1,644.87	591.27	316.75	20
20	1,169.37	530.73	297.37	10
21	1,212.87	541.34	272.77	13
22	1,304.37	492.20	314.35	11
23	1,477.62	546.34	295.53	15
24	1,593.87	590.02	293.79	19
25	1,134.87	505.32	277.05	11

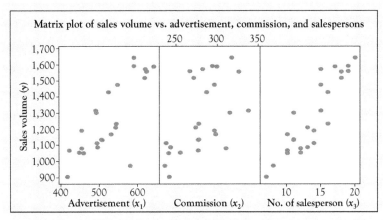

Figure 5.9 Side-by-side scatterplots of y versus x_1, x_2, x_3

Table 5.12 MINITAB regression output

```
Regression analysis: Sales volume versus advertisement, commission, no. of salespersons
The regression equation is
Sales volume (y) = -407 + 1.32 Advertisement(x₁) + 1.94
                       Commission(x₂)+ 32.4 No. of salespersons(x₃)


Predictor               Coef  SE Coef      T      P
Constant              -407.4    191.8  -2.12  0.046
Advertisement(x₁)     1.3191   0.3072   4.29  0.000
Commission(x₂)        1.9357   0.5908   3.28  0.004
No. of salespersons(x₃) 32.404  6.398   5.06  0.000


S = 72.9022   R-Sq = 91.1%   R-Sq(adj) = 89.8%


Analysis of Variance
Source          DF       SS       MS      F      P
Regression       3  1,137,364  379,121  71.33  0.000
Residual error  21    111,609    5,315
Total           24  1,248,974


Source               DF  Seq SS
Advertisement(x₁)     1  816,537
Commission(x₂)        1  184,515
No. of salespersons(x₃) 1  136,313
```

Refer to the side-by-side scatterplots in Figure 5.9, the MINITAB regression outputs in Table 5.12, the Excel output in Table 5.13, and answer the following questions.

Table 5.13 Excel regression output

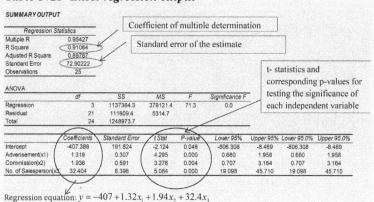

Regression equation: $y = -407 + 1.32x_1 + 1.94x_2 + 32.4x_3$

a. Interpret the scatterplots. Do you think a multiple linear model of the first order is appropriate for this data?

b. Refer to the MINITAB output or the Excel regression output and write the regression equation.

c. Interpret the meaning of the regression equation in part (b).

d. Use the MINITAB or Excel regression output to test the hypothesis that each of the independent variables: advertisement, commission paid, and the number of salespersons is significant. Use a 5% level of significance. What conclusion can be drawn from the results of these tests?

e. Refer to the MINITAB or Excel output. What percent of variation in sales volume has been explained by the regression? or What is the coefficient of determination? What is adjusted r^2? Interpret the meanings of r^2 and r^2-adjusted.

f. Conduct the F-test for the overall significance of the regression using the "*Analysis of Variance*" or the ANOVA table in either regression output table. Use a 5% level of significance. What conclusion can be drawn from the result of F-test for overall fit?

g. What are the values of residuals or the errors? Create the residual plots to check the adequacy of this regression model. Check whether all the assumptions of regression are satisfied using the residual plots.

Solution:

a. The side-by-side scatterplots shown in Figure 5.9 can be used to examine the bivariate relationships between y and x_1, y and x_2, and y and x_3. All the independent variables: advertisement (x_1), commission paid (x_2), and number of salespersons (x_3) appear to have strong linear relationship with the sales volume (y). It is evident that a first-order multiple linear regression model of the form:

$$y = b_0 + b_1 x_1 + b_2 x_2 + b_3 x_3$$

will provide a good fit to the data and can be used to predict the sales volume (y).

b. From the MINITAB regression output in Table 5.12, the regression equation is:

Sales volume (y) = –407 + 1.32 advertisement (x_1) + 1.94 commission (x_2) + 32.4 no. of salespersons (x_3)

or $\hat{y} = -407 + 1.32 x_1 + 1.94 x_2 + 32.4 x_3$

The regression equation can also be obtained from the Excel regression output in Table 5.13. In this table, refer to the column "*coefficients*," which has the same values as obtained in the preceding regression equation.

c. The regression equation in part (b) is interpreted as an estimate of mean sales volume and can be interpreted in the following way. The sales volume y is an estimate of a given level of advertisement dollars, commission paid, and number of sales persons. To be specific, the regression equation tells that for each unit increase in advertisement dollars (or each \$100 increase), the sales volume goes up by 1.32 (\$1,320) when the other variables are held constant. The other variables can be interpreted in a similar way. It is clear that for each unit increase in commissions paid while keeping the other variables constant; and for each increase in salesperson while keeping the advertisement and commissions fixed, the sales volume increases by $1,940 and $32,400, respectively.

d. The first hypothesis is to test whether the *variable advertising dollars* (x_1) is significant. This test is explained as follows.

Steps for testing the significance of the first variable, advertising dollars (x_1).

Step 1: The null and alternate hypotheses are:

$$H_0 : \beta_1 = 0$$

$$H_1 : \beta_1 \neq 0$$

where β_1 is the coefficient of "Advertisement."

Step 2: Specify the test statistic value (from the T column of MINITAB computer output or *t*-statistic from the Excel output)
The test statistic value, t for *advertisement* is 4.29. Therefore,

Test statistic value = 4.29

Step 3: Determine the critical values for the test:

$$t_{\alpha/2, n-k-1} = t_{0.025, 21} = \pm 2.080$$

where n = number of observations, k = number of independent variables; therefore, $t_{\alpha/2, n-k-1} = t_{0.025, 25-3-1} = t_{0.025, 21} = \pm 2.080$, which is the *t*-value with 21 DF for a two-tailed test with a 5% level of significance.

Step 4: Specify the decision rule for the test

Reject H_0 if $t > 2.080$
or if $t < -2.080$

Step 5: Make a decision and state your conclusion
Decision: Since $t = 4.29$ is greater than the critical value 2.080; therefore, reject H_0.
Conclusion: Advertisement is a significant variable and can contribute in predicting the sales volume.

Method 2: **Use the *p*-value approach to test the hypothesis**

Decision rule: If $p \geq \alpha$, do not reject H_0

$$\text{If } p < \alpha, \text{ reject } H_0$$

The *p*-value for advertisement can be read from either the computer output, MINITAB, or Excel (Table 5.12 or 5.13). This value is

$$p = 0.000$$

Since $p = 0.000 < \alpha = 0.05$; reject H_0.

Test for the significance of the second variable, commission paid (x_2)

We test the following hypotheses:

$$H_0 : \beta_2 = 0$$

$$H_1 : \beta_2 \neq 0$$

where β_2 is the coefficient of "Commission."

Use the *p*-value approach to test the hypothesis using the following decision rule:

Decision rule: If $p \geq \alpha$, do not reject H_0.

If $p < \alpha$, reject H_0.

The *p*-value for the variable *commission* can be read from either the MINITAB or Excel table. This value is 0.004 or,

$$p = 0.004$$

Since $p = 0.000 < \alpha = 0.05$, therefore, reject H_0.

Conclusion: Commission is a significant variable and is related to the sales volume.

Test for the significance of the third variable, number of salespersons (x_3)

Test the hypotheses:

$$H_0 : \beta_3 = 0$$

$$H_1 : \beta_3 \neq 0$$

where β_3 is the coefficient of "number of salespersons."

Using the *p*-value approach, the decision rule can be written as:

$$\text{If } p \geq \alpha, \text{ do not reject } H_0$$
$$\text{If } p < \alpha, \text{ reject } H_0$$

The *p*-value for *number of salespersons* from the computer output:

$$p = 0.000$$

Since $p = 0.000 < \alpha = 0.05$, therefore, reject H_0.

Conclusion: Number of salespersons is a significant variable and is related to the sales volume.

   e. From the MINITAB Regression output Table 5.12 or the Excel output Table 5.13, the r^2 value is 91.1% or

$$r^2 = 91.1\% \text{ (or, } 0.911)$$

This means that approximately 91% of the variation in the sales volume (*y*) has been explained by the regression. In other words, the model explains 91.1% of the variation. The unexplained or the variation due to the error is 8.9%. Note that the closer r^2 is to 1.0 or 100%, the stronger is the model.

The adjusted r^2

The adjusted r^2 is the coefficient of multiple determination adjusted for the independent or predictor variables and the sample size. This value is calculated using Equation 5.11 outlined earlier. The R^2-adjusted is given by:

$$r^2 - adj = 1 - \left[(1 - R^2) \frac{(n-1)}{n-k-1} \right] \tag{5.26}$$

where r^2 is the coefficient of multiple determination, *n* is the number of observations or the sample size, and *k* is the number of independent variables in the model. For our example problem, $r^2 = 91.1\%$, $n = 25$, and $k = 3$. Substituting these values in Equation 5.26, we get:

$$r^2 - adj = 1 - \left[(1 - 0.911) \frac{(25-1)}{25-3-1} \right] = 0.898$$

This value can be read from either computer output Table 5.12 or 5.13. The reported value in the MINITAB computer printout is:

$$R\text{-}Sq(adj.) = 89.8\%$$

This value of adjusted r^2 is used in comparing two regression models that have the same response variable but different numbers of independent or predictor variables. The adjusted r^2 value of 89.8% means that 89.8% of the variability in the sales volume y can be explained by this model, which is adjusted for the number of predictor variables k and the sample size n.

f. The hypotheses for the F-test for overall fit of the regression is:

$$H_0 : \beta_1 = \beta_2 = \beta_3 = 0$$

H_1 : at least one of the coefficients (β_i) is not equal to zero.

Method 1

This test is done using the ANOVA table in the regression output of MINITAB or Excel. The ANOVA table from the Excel is reproduced in Table 5.14.

The critical value for the test can be obtained from the F-table.

The critical value:

$$F_{k,n-k-1,\alpha} = F_{5,21,0.05} = 3.07 \text{ (from the } F\text{-table)}$$

The test statistic value:

$$F = 71.33 \text{ (from the ANOVA table)}$$

Table 5.14 The ANOVA table reproduced from the Excel regression output

	df	SS	MS	F	Significance F
Regression	3	1137364.34	379121.45	71.33	0.00
Residual	21	111609.40	5314.73		
Total	24	1248973.74			

Decision rule:

$$\text{Reject } H_0 \text{ if } F > F_{\text{critical}} = 3.07$$

Decision:

Since $F = 71.33 > F_{\text{critical}} = 3.07$, reject H_0 (the regression overall is significant).

Method 2

Use the p-value approach.

Decision rule: If $p \geq \alpha$, do not reject H_0

If $p < \alpha$, reject H_0

The p-value from the ANOVA table shown previously is 0.000. (Reported as Significance F-value in the Excel output previously.)

Since, $p = 0.000 < \alpha = 0.05$, reject H_0.

Conclusion from the F-test:

From the F-test, we can draw conclusion regarding the overall significance of regression that at least one of the coefficients $(\beta_1, \beta_2, \beta_3)$ is not equal to zero. This means that at least one of the variables (x_1, x_2, x_3) is important in explaining the variation in the sales volume (y).

g. **Residuals**:

A residual is the difference between the actual y value and the corresponding estimated value $\hat{y}$ for a given value of x, or the residual:

$$e = (y_i - \hat{y})$$

Table 5.15 shows the calculated residuals for the data of this problem (see Table 5.11 for the actual data). We have explained the calculation of residual for the first data value (refer to the first row of Table 5.15 that shows residual (RESI)). The residuals for other data values are calculated in a similar way.

Sample calculation of residual: Refer to the underlined row in Table 5.15.

The columns labeled y and x_1, x_2, x_3 are the actual data values. The estimated regression equation determined earlier for this problem is:

$$\hat{y} = -407 + 1.32x_1 + 1.94x_2 + 32.4x_3$$

Table 5.15 Residuals for the pharmaceutical company data

Row	(y)	(x₁)	(x₂)	(x₃)	FITS	RESI
1	973.62	580.17	235.48	8	1,072.99	-99.369
2	903.12	414.67	240.78	7	832.52	70.595
3	1,067.37	420.48	276.07	10	1,005.71	61.659
4	1,193.37	454.59	295.70	14	1,218.32	-24.949
5	1,429.62	524.05	286.67	16	1,357.28	72.344
6	1,557.87	623.77	325.66	18	1,629.10	-71.231
7	1,590.12	641.89	298.82	17	1,568.65	21.473
8	1,081.62	453.03	310.19	12	1,179.50	-97.882
9	1,088.37	495.76	242.91	13	1,138.04	-49.670
10	1,132.62	506.73	275.88	11	1,151.52	-18.903
11	1,314.87	490.35	337.14	15	1,378.11	-63.241
12	1,562.37	624.24	266.30	19	1,547.22	15.148
13	1,050.12	459.56	240.13	10	987.69	62.425
14	1,055.37	447.03	254.18	12	1,063.17	-7.799
15	1,112.37	493.96	237.49	14	1,157.58	-45.208
16	1,235.37	543.84	276.70	16	1,364.08	-128.713
17	1,518.12	618.38	271.14	18	1,516.46	1.663
18	1,574.37	620.50	281.94	15	1,442.95	131.422
19	1,644.87	591.27	316.75	20	1,633.79	11.081
20	1,169.37	530.73	297.37	10	1,192.38	-23.007
21	1,212.87	541.34	272.77	13	1,255.97	-43.097
22	1,304.37	492.20	314.35	11	1,206.82	97.548
23	1,477.62	546.34	295.53	15	1,371.43	106.194
24	1,593.87	590.02	293.79	19	1,555.29	38.577
25	1,134.87	505.32	277.05	11	1,151.93	-17.058

This equation can be used to calculate the estimated (predicted) value of y when $x_1 = 580.17$, $x_2 = 235.48$, and $x_3 = 8$.

$$\hat{y} = -407 + 1.32(580.17) + 1.94(235.48) + 32.4(8) = 1072.99$$

This value is reported under the "FITS" column. This value is commonly referred to as $\hat{y}$. The residual for this data value is the difference between the actual y value and the corresponding estimated value $\hat{y}$ or

$$e = (y_i - \hat{y}) = 973.62 - 1072.99 = -99.369$$

This is the residual or the error for the first value reported under the "RESI" column. The residual for other values are calculated in a similar way.

Residual Analysis
Figure 5.10 shows the residual plots for this regression model. The plots are created using MINITAB and are explained as follows.

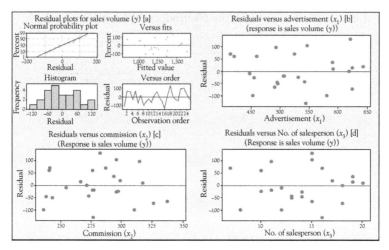

Figure 5.10 Residual plots for the pharmaceutical company data

Figure 5.10(a)—the four plots under residual plots show the normal probability plot of residuals, plot of residuals versus Fits, histogram of residuals, and residuals versus the order of the data. Figure 5.10(b), (c), and (d) are the plots of residuals versus each of the independent variables.

The **assumptions** of regression can be checked using the plot of residuals. The regression analysis is based on the following assumptions:

(a) Linearity
(b) Normality assumption
(c) Independence of errors
(d) Equal variance

Checking the Linearity Assumption

The **linearity** assumption means that the relationship between y and the independent variables is linear. To evaluate the linearity assumption, the plot of residuals versus the independent variable x is used. If the linear model is appropriate for the data, there will be no apparent pattern visible on the plots of residuals and each of the independent variables. If the relationship between x and y is not linear, the residual plot will show a relationship (pattern) between the x_i values and the residuals, e_i.

Refer to the plots in Figure 5.10(b), (c), and (d). These are the plots of residuals versus each of the independent variables: advertisement (x_1), commission paid (x_2), and number of salespersons (x_3). None of these plots show any pattern indicating that the linearity assumption holds.

Checking the Normality Assumption

The normality assumption requires that the errors have a normal or approximately normal distribution. This can be checked in several ways, such as, by constructing (1) a histogram of residuals, (2) a box plot, or (3) a normal probability plot of residuals. Refer to the normal probability plot and also the histogram of residuals in Figure 5.10(a). The plotted points in the normal probability plot fall close to the straight line. Also, the histogram of residuals shows an approximate symmetrical pattern. These two plots indicate that the residuals have approximately normal distribution and the normality assumption is not violated.

Checking the Independence of Errors Assumption

The independence of errors can be checked by plotting the errors or the residuals in the order or sequence in which the data were collected. The plot of residuals versus the order of data should show no pattern or apparent relationship (e.g., an increasing or decreasing trend) between the consecutive residuals. The plot of residuals versus order in Figure 5.10(a) shows the residuals plotted in the sequence in which the data were collected. This plot is random and does not show any pattern, which is an indication that the errors or the residuals are independent.

Checking the Equality of Variance Assumption

The equality of variance assumption requires that the errors are constant for all values of x or the variability of y values is the same for both the low and high values of x. This can be checked by plotting the residuals with x values. In cases where the equality of variance assumption is violated, the plot of residuals versus the x values would show a plot similar to

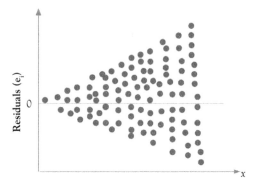

Figure 5.11 **Plot of residuals versus x values showing a violation of**
equal variance assumption

Figure 5.11. This plot shows that the variability of the residuals increases
as x increases. This demonstrates a lack of homogeneity in the variances
of y values at each level of x.

Conclusion: None of the plots indicate the violation of any assumptions on which the regression model is based. The residual analysis shows
that the model is adequate.

Summary

This chapter extended the concept of the simple linear regression model
and provided an in-depth analysis of the multiple regression model—one
of the most widely used prediction techniques used in data analysis and
decision making. We explored the multiple regression model to establish the relationship between a response variable, and two or more independent variables or the predictors. The chapter outlined the difference
between the simple and multiple regression models, provided an in-depth
analysis of multiple regression model using computer software. The high-
light of this chapter is the computer analysis and interpretation of multiple regression models. Several examples of matrix plots were presented.
These plots are helpful in the initial stages of model building. Using the
computer results, the following key features of multiple regression model
were explained: (a) the multiple regression equation and its interpretation; (b) the standard error of the estimate—a measure used to check
the utility of the model and to provide a measure of reliability of the

prediction made from the model; (c) the coefficient of multiple determination r^2 that explains the variability in the response y, explained by the independent variables used in the model; and (d) the adjusted-r^2. Besides these, we discussed the hypothesis tests using the computer results. Stepwise instructions were provided to conduct the F-test and t-tests. The overall significance of the regression model is tested using the F-test. The t-test is conducted on individual predictor or the independent variable to determine the significance of that variable. Both these tests were conducted using computer results.

Using the computer software, we also demonstrated the computation of confidence and prediction intervals for the given values of the independent variables x_1, x_2, and x_3 and provided interpretation of these intervals. The effect of multicollinearity and detection of multicollinearity using computer was discussed with examples. Finally, a detailed analysis of multiple regression model was presented. Residual analysis was presented to check whether the assumptions of regression were satisfied.

CHAPTER 6

Model Building and Computer Analysis

Introduction to Model Building

In the previous chapters, we discussed simple and multiple regression where we provided detailed analysis of these techniques including the analysis and interpretation of computer results. In both the simple and multiple regression models, the relationship among the variables is linear. In this chapter we provide an introduction to model building and nonlinear regression models. By model building, we mean selecting the model that will provide a good fit to a set of data, and the one that will provide a good estimate of the response or the dependent variable y that is related to independent variables or factors $x_1, x_2, \ldots, x_n$. It is important to choose the right model for the data.

In regression analysis, the dependent or the response variable is usually quantitative. The independent variables may be either quantitative or qualitative. The quantitative variable is one that assumes numerical values or can be expressed as numbers. The qualitative variable may not assume numerical values.

In experimental situations we often encounter both the quantitative and qualitative variables. In the model building examples, we will show later how to deal with qualitative independent variables.

Model with a Single Quantitative Independent Variable

The models relating the dependent variable y to a single quantitative independent variable x are derived from the polynomial of the form:

$$y = b_0 + b_1 x + b_2 x^2 + b_3 x^3 + \ldots + b_n x^n \qquad (6.1)$$

In Equation 6.1, n is an integer and $b_0, b_1, \ldots, b_n$ are unknown parameters that must be estimated.

(a) First-order model

The first-order model is given by:

$$y = b_0 + b_1 x$$

or

$$y = b_0 + b_1 x_1 + b_2 x_2 + b_3 x_3 + \ldots + b_n x_n \qquad (6.2)$$

where $b_0 = y$-intercept, b_i = regression coefficients.

(b) Second-order model

A second-order model can be written as:

$$y = b_0 + b_1 x + b_2 x^2 \qquad (6.3)$$

Equation 6.3 is a parabola in which:

$b_0 = y$-intercept, b_1 = a change in the value of b_1 shifts the parabola to the left or right; increasing the value of b_1 causes the parabola to shift to the left, b_2 = rate of curvature.

The second-order model is a parabola. If $b_2 > 0$ the parabola opens up; if $b_2 < 0$, the parabola opens down. The two cases are shown in Figure 6.1.

(c) Third-order model

A third-order model can be written as:

$$y = b_0 + b_1 x + b_2 x^2 + b_3 x^3 \qquad (6.4)$$

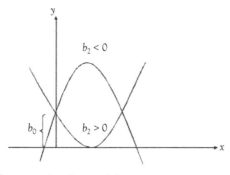

Figure 6.1 The second-order model

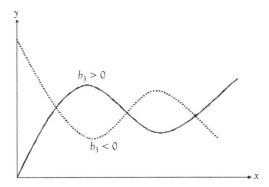

Figure 6.2 The third-order model

b_0 : y-intercept and b_3 : controls the rate of reversal of the curvature of curve.

A second-order model has no reversal in curvature. In a second-order model, the y value either continues to increase or decrease as x increases and produces either a trough or a peak. A third-order model produces one reversal in curvature and produces one peak and one trough. Reversals in curvature are not very common but can be modeled using third- or higher order polynomial. The graph of an nth-order polynomial contains ($n - 1$) peaks and troughs. Figure 6.2 shows the graph of a third-order polynomial. In real-world situation, the second-order model is perhaps the most useful.

Example 6.1: A Quadratic (Second-Order) Model

The life of an electronic component is believed to be related to the temperature in the operating environment. Table 6.1 shows 25 observations (**Data File: COMP_LIFE**) that show the life of the components (in hours) and the corresponding operating temperature (in °F). We would like to fit a model to predict the life of the component. In this case, the life of the component is the dependent variable (y) and the operating temperature is the independent variable (x).

Figure 6.3 shows the scatterplot of the data in Table 6.1. From the scatterplot, we can see that the data can be well approximated by a quadratic model.

Table 6.1 Life of electronic components

Obs	x (Temp.)	y (Life)
1	99	141.0
2	101	136.7
3	100	145.7
4	113	194.3
5	72	101.5
6	93	121.4
7	94	123.5
8	89	118.4
9	95	137.0
10	111	183.2
11	72	106.6
12	76	97.5
13	105	156.9
14	84	111.2
15	102	158.2
16	103	155.1
17	92	119.7
18	81	105.9
19	73	101.3
20	97	140.1
21	105	148.6
22	90	116.4
23	94	121.5
24	79	108.9
25	91	110.1

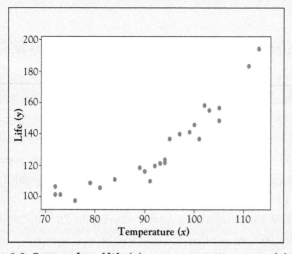

Figure 6.3 Scatterplot of life (y) versus operating temp. (x)

Table 6.2 Computer results of second-order model

```
Results for: QUADMOD.MTW
 Regression Analysis: Life (y) versus Temp. (x), x*x


The regression equation is
Life (y) = 433 - 8.89 Temp. (x) + 0.0598 x*x


Predictor       Coef   SE Coef      T      P
Constant      433.01     61.84   7.00  0.000
Temp. (x)     -8.891      1.374  -6.47  0.000
x*x         0.059823   0.007549   7.93  0.000


S = 5.37620    R-Sq = 95.9%    R-Sq(adj) = 95.6%


Analysis of Variance
Source          DF        SS       MS       F      P
Regression       2   15,011.8  7,505.9  259.69  0.000
Residual Error  22     635.9      28.9
Total           24   15,647.7
```

We used MINITAB and Excel to fit a second-order model to the data. The instructions for running the second-order model using MINITAB are provided in ***Appendix A_Table A.15***. The analysis of the computer results is presented in Table 6.2.

Second-Order Model Using MINITAB

A second-order model was fitted using MINITAB. The regression output of the model is shown in Table 6.3.

A quadratic model in MINITAB can also be run using the fitted line plot option. The results of the quadratic model using this option provide a fitted line plot (shown in Figure 6.4). The regression output using the fitted line option is slightly different from the conventional regression model. Table 6.3 shows the regression output using the fitted line option plot in MINITAB. Note that the regression output using the conventional regression model shown in Table 6.2 shows more details.

Table 6.3 Regression analysis table

```
Polynomial Regression Analysis: y versus x
The regression equation is

y = 433 - 8.891 x + 0.05982 x^2

S = 5.37620      R-Sq = 95.9%      R-Sq(adj) = 95.6%


Analysis of Variance

Source             DF        SS          MS         F       P
Regression          2    15,011.8    7,505.89   259.687   0.000
Error              22       635.9      28.90
Total              24    15,647.7


Source      DF     Seq SS         F       P
Linear       1    13,196.4    123.821   0.000
Quadratic    1     1,815.4     62.808   0.000
```

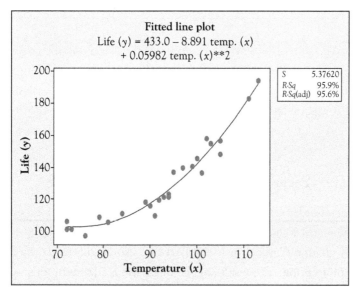

Figure 6.4 Regression plot with equation

While running the quadratic model, the data values and residuals can also be stored. Table 6.4 shows the actual data and residuals. The plots of residuals are explained in the next section.

Table 6.4 Data with stored residuals and fitted values

Row	x	y	RESI1	FITS1	COEF1
1	99	141.0	1.8501	139.150	433.006
2	101	136.7	-8.5977	145.298	-8.891
3	100	145.7	3.5361	142.164	0.060
4	113	194.3	2.0650	192.235	
5	72	101.5	-1.4959	102.996	
6	93	121.4	-2.1779	123.578	
7	94	123.5	-2.3741	125.874	
8	89	118.4	2.8105	115.590	
9	95	137.0	8.7100	128.290	
10	111	183.2	-0.0156	183.216	
11	72	106.6	3.6041	102.996	
12	76	97.5	-5.3483	102.848	
13	105	156.9	-2.1291	159.029	
14	84	111.2	2.9039	108.296	
15	102	158.2	9.6489	148.551	
16	103	155.1	3.1759	151.924	
17	92	119.7	-1.7013	121.401	
18	81	105.9	0.5442	105.356	
19	73	101.3	-1.4795	102.780	
20	97	140.1	6.6194	133.481	
21	105	148.6	-10.4291	159.029	
22	90	116.4	-1.0072	117.407	
23	94	121.5	-4.3741	125.874	
24	79	108.9	4.9061	103.994	
25	91	110.1	-9.2444	119.344	

Residual Plots for the Example 6.1 Using MINITAB

Figure 6.5 shows the residual plots for this quadratic model. The residual plots are useful in checking the assumptions of the model and the model adequacy.

The analysis of residual plots for this model is similar to that of simple and multiple regression models. The investigation of the plots shows that the normality assumption is met. The plot of residuals versus the fitted values shows a random pattern indicating that the quadratic model fitted to the data is adequate.

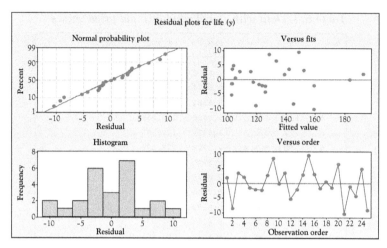

Figure 6.5 Residual plots for the quadratic model example

Running a Second-Order Model Using Excel

Unlike MINITAB, Excel does not provide an option to run a quadratic model of the form:

$$y = b_0 + b_1 x + b_2 x^2$$

However, we can run a quadratic regression model by calculating the x^2 column from the x column in the data file. To run the quadratic regression model, enter the data from Table 6.1 in columns A and B of Excel worksheet, where column A contains the response variable y and column B contains the predictor or the x variable. Next, create the x^2 column by typing the following expression in cell C2: = B2*B2 and copying this formula into the cells C3 to C26. This will create the x^2 column. Label column C with $x{**}2$. Part of the data file is shown in Table 6.5.

Once the data file is created, follow the steps in Table 6.6 to run the quadratic model. The data are shown in the file: **COMP_LIFE** and also in Table 6.1 shown earlier.

The Excel computer results are shown in Table 6.7.

Table 6.5 Part of Excel data file

	A	B	C
1	Life (y)	Temp. (x)	x**2
2	141	99	9801
3	136.7	101	10201
4	145.7	100	10000
5	194.3	113	12769
6	101.5	72	5184
7	121.4	93	8649
8	123.5	94	8836

Table 6.6 Steps for quadratic regression in Excel

1. Click on the Data tab.
2. Click Data Analysis.
3. Select Regression.
4. Select Life (y) for Input y range and the other two columns x, and $x**2$ for the input x range (make sure to select the first row or the row with the labels).
5. Check the Labels box.
6. Click on the circle next to Output Range, click on the box (cell)next to output range and specify where you want to store the output by clicking a blank cell in the worksheet.
7. You may check the boxes under residuals and normal probability plot as desired.
8. Click OK.

Table 6.7 Excel computer output for the quadratic model

SUMMARY OUTPUT

Regression Statistics	
Multiple R	0.97947
R Square	0.95936
Adjusted R Square	0.95567
Standard Error	5.37620
Observations	25

ANOVA

	df	SS	MS	F	Significance F
Regression	2	15011.7720	7505.8860	259.6872	0.0000
Residual	22	635.8784	28.9036		
Total	24	15647.6504			

	Coefficients	Standard Error	t Stat	P-value	Lower 95%	Upper 95%	Lower 95.0%	Upper 95.0%
Intercept	433.0063	61.8367	7.0024	0.0000	304.7648	561.2478	304.7648	561.2478
Temp. (x)	-8.8908	1.3743	-6.4691	0.0000	-11.7410	-6.0405	-11.7410	-6.0405
x**2	0.0598	0.0075	7.9251	0.0000	0.0442	0.0755	0.0442	0.0755

Analysis of Computer Results of Tables 6.3 and 6.7

Refer to MINITAB output in Table 6.3 or the Excel computer output in Table 6.7. The prediction equation from either table can be written using the coefficients column. The equation is:

$$\hat{y} = 433 - 8.89x + 0.0598x^2$$

In the Excel output, the prediction equation can be read from the "coefficients" column.

The r^2 value is 95.9%, which is an indication of a strong model. It indicates that 95.9% of the variation in y can be explained by the variation in x and 4.1% of the variation is unexplained or due to error. The equation can be used to predict the life of the components at a specified temperature.

We can also test a hypothesis to determine if the second-order term in our model, in fact, contributes to the prediction of y. The null and alternate hypotheses to be tested for this can be expressed as:

$$H_0 : \beta_2 = 0$$
$$H_1 : \beta_2 \neq 0$$

(6.5)

The test statistic for this test is given by

$$t = \frac{b_2}{s_{b_2}}$$

The test statistic value is calculated by the computer and is shown in Table 6.7. In this table, the t-value is reported in $x^{**}2$ row and under t-stat column. This value is 7.93. Thus,

$$t = \frac{b_2}{s_{b_2}} = 7.93$$

The **critical value** for the test is

$$t_{n-k-1,\alpha/2} = t_{22,0.025} = 2.074$$

(Note: t_{n-k-1} is the t-value from the t-table for $(n - k - 1)$ degrees of freedom where n is the number of observations and k is the number of independent variables.

For our example, $n = 25$, $k = 2$, and the level of significance, $\alpha = 0.05$. Using these values, the critical value or the t-value from the t-table for 22 degrees of freedom and $\alpha = 0.025$ is 2.074. Since the calculated value of t is 7.93, which is greater than the critical value that is,

$$t = 7.93 > t_{critical} = 2.074$$

We reject the null hypothesis and conclude that the second-order term in fact contributes to the prediction of the life of components (y). Note: we could also have tested the following hypotheses:

$$H_0 : \beta = 0$$
$$H_1 : \beta > 0$$

which would determine that the value of $b_2 = 0.0598$ in the prediction equation is large enough to conclude that the life of the components increases at an increasing rate with temperature. This hypothesis will have the same test statistic and can be tested at $\alpha = 0.05$.

Therefore, our conclusion is that the mean component life increases at an increasing rate of temperature and the second-order term in our model, in fact, is significant and contributes to the prediction of y.

Comparing the Quadratic Model to the Linear Model

We fitted a ***linear model*** of the form $y = b_0 + b_1 x_1$ using MINITAB for the data in Table 6.1. Figure 6.6 shows the plot with fitted prediction equation. The regression output is shown in Table 6.8, and the plots of residual are shown in Figure 6.7.

In Figure 6.6, the r^2 value is 84.3% (it is a drop in r^2 value of 95.9% in the quadratic model when compared to the r^2 value of the quadratic model in Table 6.3). Also, refer to the Residual versus Fitted values plot in Figure 6.7. This plot shows a pattern that is an indication that the linear model is inadequate for the given data.

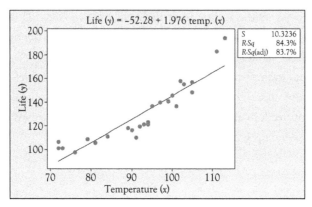

Figure 6.6 Fitted line plot

Table 6.8 The regression output for the linear model

```
The regression equation is
y = -52.2758 + 1.97646x


S = 10.3236          R-Sq = 84.3%          R-Sq(adj) = 83.7%


Analysis of Variance


Source          DF          SS          MS          F          P
Regression      1           13,196.4    13,196.4    123.821    0.000
Error           23          2,451.3     106.6
Total           24          15,647.7
```

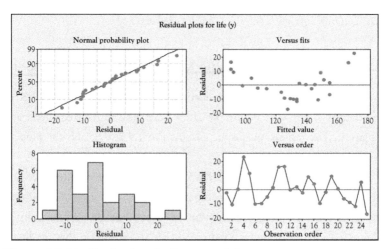

Figure 6.7 Residuals plots for linear model

Comparing the residual versus the fitted value plot for the linear model in Figure 6.7 to the corresponding residual plot for the quadratic model of Figure 6.5, we see no apparent pattern for the residual versus the fitted value plot for the quadratic model. This is an indication that the quadratic model is an appropriate model for the problem.

Example 6.2: Quadratic (Second-Order) Model

The data in Table 6.9 (*Data File: YIELD.MTW*) shows the yield of a chemical process at different temperatures. The fitted line plot of the temperature and yield in Figure 6.8 indicates a nonlinear relationship. The plot shows that the data can be well approximated by a quadratic model.

Table 6.9 Yield at different temperatures

Obs.	Temp.(x)	Yield (y)	Obs.	Temp.(x)	Yield (y)
1	50	12,506	26	175	22,890
2	55	12,485	27	180	23,610
3	60	14,513	28	185	22,281
4	65	14,301	29	190	21,905
5	70	16,630	30	195	22,481
6	75	17,900	31	200	20,006
7	80	17,680	32	205	20,500
8	85	17,300	33	210	19,900
9	90	19,900	34	215	18,281
10	95	19,520	35	220	17,610
11	100	21,020	36	225	17,890
12	105	20,500	37	230	16,106
13	110	22,900	38	235	15,281
14	115	23,300	39	240	15,410
15	120	21,606	40	245	14,500
16	125	24,890	41	250	14,520
17	130	21,118	42	255	16,681
18	135	22,281	43	260	13,516
19	140	23,410	44	265	6,281
20	145	24,480	45	270	10,119
21	150	22,530	46	275	7,890
22	155	21,490	47	280	15,610
23	160	23,406	48	285	7,280
24	165	24,290	49	290	5,906
25	170	22,106	50	295	8,481

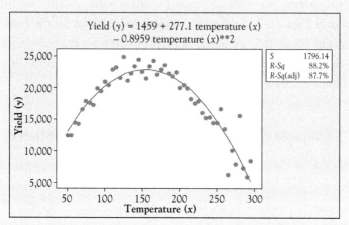

Figure 6.8 *Plot showing the points and the fitted curve*

a. Use MINITAB to run a quadratic model to the data.
b. Use Excel to run this quadratic model. Enter the x and y values from Table 6.9 in columns A and B of Excel then create column C by squaring the x values. Label this column x^2 (or $x**2$) then follow the instructions in Example 6.1 (Running Second-Order Model using Excel).
c. Show the fitted quadratic model and the regression output from MINITAB or Excel.
d. What is the prediction equation relating yield (y) and the temperature (x).
   What is the coefficient of determination? What does it tell you about the model?

Solution:

(a) and (b): The regression output from MINITAB is shown in Table 6.10. Similar result can be obtained using Excel.

(c) The fitted quadratic model with the regression equation is shown in Figure 6.8.

(d) The prediction equation from the regression output in Table 6.10 is

Yield (y) = 1,459 + 277 Temperature (x) − 0.896 $x*x$

Table 6.10 Regression output for Example 6.2

```
Results for: YIELD1.MTW


Regression Analysis: Yield (y) versus Temperature (x), x*x


The regression equation is
Yield (y) = 1,459 + 277 Temperature (x) - 0.896 x*x


Predictor           Coef    SE Coef        T      P
Constant           1,459      1,493     0.98  0.334
Temperature (x)   277.12      19.16    14.47  0.000
x*x              -0.89585    0.05458  -16.41  0.000


S = 1,796.14    R-Sq = 88.2%    R-Sq(adj) = 87.7%


Analysis of Variance


Source            DF          SS         MS       F      P
Regression         2  1134859671  567429836  175.89  0.000
Residual Error    47   151628370    3226136
Total             49  1286488041
Source            DF      Seq SS
Temperature (x)    1   265772263
x*x                1   869087408
```

or

$$\hat{y} = 1459 + 277x - 0.896x^2$$

The coefficient of determination, R^2 is 88.2% (reported as $R\text{-}Sq$ = 88.2%) in Table 6.10. This tells us that 88.2% of the variation in y is explained by the regression and 11.8% of the variation is unexplained or due to error.

Summary

This chapter provided an introduction to model building. We explained the first-order, second-order, and third-order models. Unlike the simple and multiple regression models, where the relationship among the variables is linear, there are situations where the relationship among the variables under study may not be linear. This chapter explained the situation where higher order and nonlinear models provide a better relationship between the response and independent variables. We provided examples of quadratic or second-order models. Scatterplots were created to select the model that would provide a good fit to a set of data and can be used to obtain a good estimate of the response or the dependent variable y that is related to the independent variables or predictors. Since the second-order or quadratic models are appropriate in many applications, we provided a detailed computer analysis of such models. The computer analysis and interpretation of computer results were explained through examples. Residual analysis was conducted to check whether the second-order model provided a good fit to the data. We also compared the second-order model to the linear model to demonstrate why the former provided a better fit to the data.

CHAPTER 7

Models with Qualitative Independent (Dummy) Variables, Interaction Models, All Subset and Stepwise Regression Models with Computer Analysis

Dummy or Indicator Variables in Multiple Regression

In regression, we often encounter qualitative or indicator variables that need to be included as one of the independent variables in the model. For example, if we are interested in building a regression model to predict the salary of male and female employees based on their education and years of experience, the variable male or female is a qualitative variable that must be included as a separate independent variable in the model. To include such qualitative variables in the model we use a *dummy* or *indicator* variable. The use of dummy or indicator variables in a regression model allows us to include qualitative variables in the model. For example, to include the sex of employees in a regression model as an independent variable, we define this variable as:

$$x_1 = \begin{cases} 1 \\ 0 \end{cases}$$

In the preceding formulation, a "1" indicates that the employee is a male and a "0" means the employee is a female. Which one of the male or female is assigned the value of 1 is arbitrary.

In general, the number of dummy or indicator variables needed is one less than the total number of indicator variables to be included in the model.

One Qualitative Independent Variable at Two Levels

Suppose we want to build a model to predict the mean salary of male and female employees. This model can be written as:

$$y = b_0 + b_1 x$$

where x is the dummy variable coded as:

$$x_1 = \begin{cases} 1 & \text{if male} \\ 0 & \text{if female} \end{cases}$$

This coding scheme will allow us to compare the mean salary for male and female employees by substituting the appropriate code in the regression equation: $y = b_0 + b_1 x$.

Suppose μ_M = mean salary for the male employees

μ_F = mean salary for the female employees

Then the mean salary for the male: $\mu_M = y = b_0 + b_1(1) = b_0 + b_1$

and the mean salary for the female: $\mu_F = y = b_0 + b_1(0) = b_0$

Thus, the mean salary for the female employees is b_0. In a 0–1 coding system, the mean response will always be b_0 for the qualitative variable that is assigned the value 0. This is also called the **base level**.

The difference in the mean salary for the male and female employees can be calculated by taking the difference $(\mu_M - \mu_F)$.

$$\mu_M - \mu_F = (b_0 + b_1) - b_0 = b_1$$

The aforementioned is the difference between the mean response for the level that is assigned the value 1 and the level that is assigned the value 0 or the base level. The mean salary for the male and female employees is shown graphically in Figure 7.1. We can also see that:

$$b_0 = \mu_F$$
$$b_1 = \mu_M - \mu_F$$

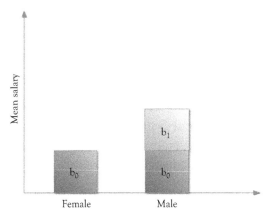

Figure 7.1 Mean salary of female and male employees

Model with One Qualitative Independent Variable at Three Levels

As an example, we would like to write a model relating the mean profit of a grocery chain. It is believed that the profit to a large extent depends on the location of the stores. Suppose that the management is interested in three specific locations where the stores are located. We will call these locations A, B, and C. In this case, the store location is a single qualitative variable that is at three levels corresponding to the three locations A, B, and C. The prediction equation relating the mean profit (y) and the three locations *can be written as*:

$$y = b_0 + b_1 x_1 + b_2 x_2$$

where

$$x_1 = \begin{cases} 1 & \text{if location B} \\ 0 & \text{if not} \end{cases}$$

$$x_2 = \begin{cases} 1 & \text{if location C} \\ 0 & \text{if not} \end{cases}$$

The variables x_1 and x_2 are known as the ***dummy variables*** that make the model function.

Explanation of the Model

Suppose, μ_A = mean profit for location A

μ_B = mean profit for location B

μ_C = mean profit for location C

If we set $x_1 = 0$ and $x_2 = 0$, we will get the mean profit for location A. Therefore, the mean value of profit y when the store location is A is:

$$\mu_A = y = b_0 + b_1(0) + b_2(0)$$

or,

$$\mu_A = b_0$$

Thus, the mean profit for location A is b_0 or

$$b_0 = \mu_A$$

Similarly, the mean profit for location B can be calculated by setting $x_1 = 1$ and $x_2 = 0$. The resulting equation is:

$$\mu_B = y = b_0 + b_1 x_1 + b_2 x_2 = b_0 + b_1(1) + b_2(0)$$

or,

$$\mu_B = b_0 + b_1$$

Since

$$b_0 = \mu_A, \text{ we can write}$$
$$\mu_B = \mu_A + b_1$$

or

$$b_1 = \mu_B - \mu_A$$

Finally, the mean profit for location C can be calculated by setting $x_1 = 0$ and $x_2 = 1$. The resulting equation is:

$$\mu_C = y = b_0 + b_1 x_1 + b_2 x_2 = b_0 + b_1(0) + b_2(1)$$

or,

$$\mu_C = b_0 + b_2$$

Since

$$b_0 = \mu_A, \text{ we can write}$$

$$\mu_C = \mu_A + b_2$$
$$b_2 = \mu_C - \mu_A$$

Thus, in the previous coding system, one qualitative independent variable is at three levels:

$$\mu_A = b_0 \quad \text{and} \quad b_1 = \mu_B - \mu_A$$
$$\mu_B = b_0 + b_1 \qquad b_2 = \mu_C - \mu_A$$
$$\mu_C = b_0 + b_2$$

where μ_A, μ_B, μ_C are the mean profits for locations A, B, and C.

---

*Note that the three levels of the qualitative variable can be described with only two dummy variables. This is because the mean of the base level (in this case location A) is accounted for by the intercept b_0. In general form, for **m** levels of qualitative variable, we need (**m**−1) dummy variables.*

The bar graph in Figure 7.2 shows the values of mean profit (y) for the three locations.

In the preceding bar chart, the height of the bar corresponding to location A is $y = b_0$. Similarly, the heights of the bars corresponding to

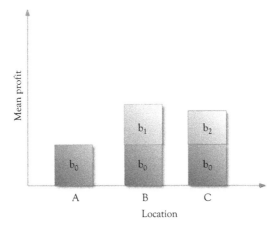

Figure 7.2 Bar chart showing the mean profit for three locations A, B, C

locations B and C are $y = b_0 + b_1$ and $y = b_0 + b_2$, respectively. Note that either b_1 or b_2, or both could be negative. In Figure 7.2, b_1 and b_2 are both positive. The general form of the model when one qualitative independent variable is at m levels is shown as follows.

General form of the model with one qualitative independent variable at m levels

The model:

$$y = b_0 + b_1 x_1 + b_2 x_2 + \ldots + b_{m-1} x_{m-1}$$

where x_i is the dummy variable for level $(i + 1)$ and

$$x_i = \begin{cases} 1 & \text{if } y \text{ is observed at level } (i+1) \\ 0 & \text{otherwise} \end{cases}$$

For the preceding system of coding

$$\mu_A = b_0$$
$$\mu_B = b_0 + b_1$$
$$\mu_C = b_0 + b_2$$
$$\mu_D = b_0 + b_3$$
$$\vdots$$

and

$$b_1 = \mu_B - \mu_A$$
$$b_2 = \mu_C - \mu_A$$
$$b_3 = \mu_D - \mu_A$$
$$\vdots$$

Example 7.1: Dummy Variables

Consider the problem of the pharmaceutical company model where the relationship between the sales volume (y) and three quantitative independent variables—advertisement dollars spent (x_1) in hundreds of dollars, commission paid to the salespersons (x_2) in hundreds of dollars, and the number of salespersons (x_3)—were investigated. The company is now interested in including different sales territories where they market the drug. The territory in which the company markets the drug is divided into three zones: zone A, B, and C. The management wants to predict the sales for the three zones separately. To do this, the variable "zone," which is a qualitative independent variable, must be included in the model. The company identified the sales volumes for the three zones along with the variables considered earlier. The data including the sales volume and the three zones are shown in the last column of Table 7.1 (*Data File: DummyVar_File1*). Since there are three zones (A, B, and C) in which the company markets the drug, we have three qualitative variables. To include these three zones in the model, we will need only two indicator or dummy variables because for three dummy variables we will

Table 7.1 Sales for different zones

Row	Sales volume (y)	Advertisement (x_1)	Commission (x_2)	No. of salespersons (x_3)	Zone
1	973.62	580.17	235.48	8	A
2	903.12	414.67	240.78	7	A
3	1067.37	420.48	276.07	10	A
4	1193.37	454.59	295.70	14	B
5	1429.62	524.05	286.67	16	C
6	1557.87	623.77	325.66	18	A
7	1590.12	641.89	298.82	17	A
8	1081.62	403.03	210.19	12	C
9	1088.37	415.76	202.91	13	C
10	1132.62	506.73	275.88	11	B
11	1314.87	490.35	337.14	15	A
12	1562.37	624.24	266.30	19	C
13	1050.12	459.56	240.13	10	C
14	1055.37	447.03	254.18	12	B
15	1112.37	493.96	237.49	14	B
16	1235.37	543.84	276.70	16	B
17	1518.12	618.38	271.14	18	A
18	1574.37	690.50	281.94	15	C
19	1644.87	591.27	316.75	20	C
20	1169.37	530.73	297.37	10	C
21	1212.87	541.34	272.77	13	B
22	1304.37	492.20	344.35	11	B
23	1477.62	546.34	295.53	15	C
24	1593.87	590.02	293.79	19	C
25	1134.87	505.32	277.05	11	B

need only two variables and use the code 0 or 1 to represent the zones. To represent the three zones, we use two dummy variables as follows:

$$x_4 = \begin{cases} 1 & \text{if zone A} \\ 0 & \text{otherwise} \end{cases} \quad x_5 = \begin{cases} 1 & \text{if zone B} \\ 0 & \text{otherwise} \end{cases}$$

In this coding system, the choice of 0 and 1 in the coding is arbitrary.

Note that, we have defined only two dummy variables—x_4 and x_5 for a total of three zones. It is not necessary to define a third dummy variable for zone C because we have the following scheme:

Zone	x_4	x_5
A	1	0
B	0	1
C	0	0

It can be shown that a third dummy variable is not necessary for all the three zones. For example, suppose a third dummy variable x_6 is introduced that is equal to 1 if the sale is from zone C. Then for each observation in the sample, the following relationship holds: $x_6 = 1 - x_4 - x_5$.

This means that this predictor variable is a linear function of other predictors. Whenever one predictor variable is a linear function of one or more predictor variables (including any constant term), then there is no solution for the least squares coefficients because of multicollinearity. Therefore, any such predictor variable must not be included in the model for the equation to be meaningful.

From the previous discussion, it follows that the regression model for the data in Table 7.1 including the variable "zone" can be written as:

$$y = b_0 + b_1 x_1 + b_2 x_2 + b_3 x_3 + b_4 x_4 + b_5 x_5$$

where (y): sales volume (y),
(x_1): advertisement dollars spent in hundreds of dollars,
(x_2): commission paid to the salespersons in hundreds of dollars,
(x_3): the numbers of salespersons, and the dummy variables:

$$x_4 = \begin{cases} 1 & \text{if zone A} \\ 0 & \text{otherwise} \end{cases} \quad x_5 = \begin{cases} 1 & \text{if zone B} \\ 0 & \text{otherwise} \end{cases}$$

Table 7.2 shows the data file for this regression model with the dummy variables. We will use both MINITAB and Excel to run this model and provide analysis of the computer results. The data can be obtained from the MINITAB data file—[**Data File: DummyVar_ File(2)**] or from the Excel data file—DummyVar_File (2).xlsx. The instructions for running this model can be found in **Appendix A_ Table A.16.**

    a. Using the MINITAB data file, run a regression model. Show your regression output.

    b. Using the Excel data file, run a regression model. Show your regression output.

Table 7.2 Data file for the model with dummy variables

Row	Volume (y) (y)	Advertisement (x_1)	Commission (x_2)	No. of salespersons (x_3)	Zone A (x_4)	Zone B (x_5)
1	973.62	580.17	235.48	8	1	0
2	903.12	414.67	240.78	7	1	0
3	1,067.37	420.48	276.07	10	1	0
4	1,193.37	454.59	295.70	14	0	1
5	1,429.62	524.05	286.67	16	0	0
6	1,557.87	623.77	325.66	18	1	0
7	1,590.12	641.89	298.82	17	1	0
8	1,081.62	403.03	210.19	12	0	0
9	1,088.37	415.76	202.91	13	0	0
10	1,132.62	506.73	275.88	11	0	1
11	1,314.87	490.35	337.14	15	1	0
12	1,562.37	624.24	266.30	19	0	0
13	1,050.12	459.56	240.13	10	0	0
14	1,055.37	447.03	254.18	12	0	1
15	1,112.37	493.96	237.49	14	0	1
16	1,235.37	543.84	276.70	16	0	1
17	1,518.12	618.38	271.14	18	1	0
18	1,574.37	690.50	281.94	15	0	0
19	1,644.87	591.27	316.75	20	0	0
20	1,169.37	530.73	297.37	10	0	0
21	1,212.87	541.34	272.77	13	0	1
22	1,304.37	492.20	344.35	11	0	1
23	1,477.62	546.34	295.53	15	0	0
24	1,593.87	590.02	293.79	19	0	0
25	1,134.87	505.32	277.05	11	0	1

c. Using the MINITAB or Excel regression output, write down the regression equation.

d. Using a 5% level of significance and the column "p" in the MINITAB regression output or "p-value" column in the Excel regression output, conduct appropriate hypotheses tests to determine that the independent variables: advertisement, commission paid, and number of sales persons are significant or they contribute in predicting the sales volume.

e. Write separate regression equations to predict the sales for each of the zones A, B, and C.

f. Refer to the given MINITAB residual plots and check that all the regression assumptions are met and the fitted regression model is adequate.

Solution:

a. The MINITAB regression output is shown in Table 7.3.

b. Table 7.4 shows the Excel regression output.

c. From the MINITAB or the Excel regression outputs in Tables 7.3 and 7.4, the regression equation is:

Sales volume $(y) = -98.2 + 0.884$ Advertisement (x_1)
$+ 1.81$ Commission $(x_2) + 33.8$ No. of salespersons $(x_3) - 67.2$ Zone A (x_4)
$- 105$ Zone B (x_5)

or

$$y = -98.2 + 0.884x_1 + 1.81x_2 + 33.8x_3 - 67.2x_4 - 105x_5$$

The regression equation from the Excel output in Table 7.4 can be written using the coefficients column.

d. The hypotheses to check the significance of each of the independent variables can be written as:

$$H_0 : \beta_j = 0 \ (x_j \text{ is not a significant variable})$$

$$H_1 : \beta_j \neq 0 \ (x_j \text{ is a significant variable})$$

Table 7.3 MINITAB regression output

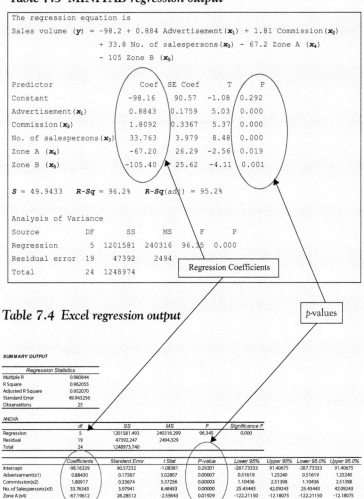

```
The regression equation is
Sales volume (y) = -98.2 + 0.884 Advertisement(x₁) + 1.81 Commission(x₂)
                   + 33.8 No. of salespersons(x₃) - 67.2 Zone A (x₄)
                   - 105 Zone B (x₅)


Predictor                    Coef    SE Coef       T       P
Constant                   -98.16      90.57   -1.08   0.292
Advertisement(x₁)          0.8843     0.1759    5.03   0.000
Commission(x₂)             1.8092     0.3367    5.37   0.000
No. of salespersons(x₃)    33.763      3.979    8.48   0.000
Zone A (x₄)                -67.20      26.29   -2.56   0.019
Zone B (x₅)               -105.40      25.62   -4.11   0.001


S = 49.9433   R-Sq = 96.2%   R-Sq(adj) = 95.2%


Analysis of Variance
Source          DF       SS      MS       F       P
Regression       5  1201581  240316   96.35   0.000
Residual error  19    47392    2494
Total           24  1248974
```

Regression Coefficients

Table 7.4 Excel regression output

p-values

SUMMARY OUTPUT

Regression Statistics	
Multiple R	0.980844
R Square	0.962055
Adjusted R Square	0.952070
Standard Error	49.943256
Observations	25

ANOVA

	df	SS	MS	F	Significance F
Regression	5	1201581.493	240316.299	96.345	0.000
Residual	19	47392.247	2494.329		
Total	24	1248973.740			

	Coefficients	Standard Error	t Stat	P-value	Lower 95%	Upper 95%	Lower 95.0%	Upper 95.0%
Intercept	-98.16329	90.57232	-1.08381	0.29201	-287.73333	91.40675	-287.73333	91.40675
Adverisement(x1)	0.88430	0.17587	5.02807	0.00007	0.51619	1.25240	0.51619	1.25240
Commission(x2)	1.80917	0.33674	5.37256	0.00003	1.10436	2.51398	1.10436	2.51398
No. of Salespersons(x3)	33.76343	3.97941	8.48453	0.00000	25.43443	42.09243	25.43443	42.09243
Zone A (x4)	-67.19612	26.28512	-2.55643	0.01929	-122.21150	-12.18075	-122.21150	-12.18075
Zone B (x5)	-105.40027	25.62300	-4.11350	0.00059	-159.02982	-51.77072	-159.02982	-51.77072

This hypothesis can be tested using the "p" column in either MINITAB or the p-value column in Excel computer results. The decision rule for the p-value approach is given by:

$$\text{If } p \geq \alpha, \text{ do not reject } H_0$$

$$\text{If } p < \alpha, \text{ reject } H_0$$

Table 7.5 Summary table

Independent variable	p-value from Table 7.3 or 7.4	Compare p to α	Decision	Significant? Yes or no
Advertisement (x_1)	0.000	$p < \alpha$	Reject H_0	Yes
Commissions (x_2)	0.000	$p < \alpha$	Reject H_0	Yes
No. of salespersons (x_3)	0.000	$p < \alpha$	Reject H_0	Yes

Table 7.5 shows the *p*-value for each of the predictor variables. Refer to MINITAB or Excel computer results in Table 7.3 or 7.4 (see the "p" or the "*p*-value" columns in these tables).

From this table it can be seen that all the three independent variables are significant.

e. As indicated, the overall regression equation is:

Sales volume $(y) = -98.2 + 0.884$ *Advertisement* (x_1)
$+ 1.81$ *Commission* $(x_2) + 33.8$ *No. of salespersons* $(x_3) - 67.2$ *Zone A* $(x_4) - 105$ *Zone B* (x_5)

Separate equations for each zone can be written from this equation as explained in the following.

Zone A: $x_4 = 1.0, x_5 = 0$

Therefore, the equation for the sales volume of Zone A can be written as

Sales volume $(y) = -98.2 + 0.884$ *Advertisement* $(x_1) + 1.81$ *Commission* (x_2)
$+ 33.8$ *No. of salespersons* $(x_3) - 67.2 (1) - 105 (0.0)$ *or,*

Sales volume $(y) = -98.2 + 0.884$ Advertisement $(x_1) + 1.81$ Commission (x_2)
$+ 33.8$ No. of salespersons $(x_3) - 67.2$ or,

Sales volume $(y) = -165.4 + 0.884$ Advertisement (x_1)
$+ 1.81$ Commission $(x_2) + 33.8$ No. of salespersons (x_3)

Similarly, the regression equations for the other two zones are shown below.

Zone B: $x_4 = 0$, $x_5 = 1.0$

Substituting these values in the overall regression equation of part (c)

Sales volume (y) = $-98.2 + 0.884$ Advertisement (x_1) + 1.81 Commission (x_2) + 33.8 No. of salespersons (x_3) – 105 or,

Sales volume (y) = $-203.2 + 0.884$ Advertisement (x_1) + 1.81 Commission (x_2) + 33.8 No. of salespersons (x_3)

Zone C: $x_4 = 0$, $x_5 = 0$

Substituting these values in the overall regression equation of part (c)

Sales volume (y) = $-98.2 + 0.884$ Advertisement (x_1) + 1.81 Commission (x_2) + 33.8 No. of salespersons (x_3)

Note that in all of the preceding equations, the slopes are same but intercepts are different.

f. The MINITAB residual plots are shown in Figure 7.3.

The residual plots in Figure 7.3 show that the normal probability plot and the histogram of residuals are approximately normally distributed. The plot of residuals versus fits does not show any pattern and is quite random indicating that the fitted linear regression model is adequate. The plot of residuals and the order of data points show no apparent pattern indicating that there is no violation of independence of error assumptions.

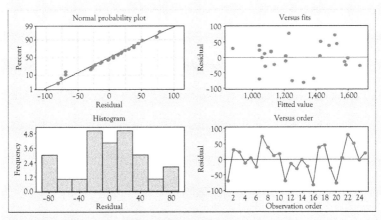

Figure 7.3 Residual plots for Example 7.1

Example 7.2: Dummy Variables

An article in the IT Salary Survey magazine recently reported an employment discrimination case in the IT industry. It compared mean salaries of male and female employees and arrived at a conclusion that the female employees earn significantly less than their male counterparts for the same job. One of the IT companies facing several discrimination law suits hired an independent consultant to look into their salary structure. The consultant collected the data on the variables (shown in Table 7.6). The variables include: y—salary (in thousands of dollars) paid to the employees, years of education (x_1), years of experience (x_2), dummy variable coded (x_3), 1 for male employees and 0 for female employees.

Table 7.6 Salary data for male and female employees

Row	Salary (y)	Years of education (x_1)	Years of experience (x_2)	Male (x_3)
1	42	10	0	1
2	40	10	2	0
3	44	12	1	0
4	56	15	3	1
5	44	12	2	0
6	45	12	3	1
7	54	12	7	1
8	43	12	2	0
9	47	10	3	1
10	51	12	4	1
11	48	12	4	0
12	49	12	5	0
13	58	16	4	0
14	60	16	6	1
15	63	16	7	1
16	58	12	7	1
17	40	8	3	0
18	48	12	4	1
19	52	12	6	0
20	56	15	7	0
21	59	15	6	1
22	62	16	8	1
23	63	16	6	1
24	62	15	8	0
25	61	16	4	1
26	62	16	5	1
27	54	12	6	0
28	43	8	3	0
29	51	12	5	0
30	65	16	7	0

A regression model was fitted using this data. Tables 7.7 and 7.8 show the MINITAB and Excel results for the data in Table 7.6 [the data files are: [*Data File: DummyVar_File (3)*], refer to the regression outputs and answer the questions that follow. Is there an evidence of discrimination in salary between the male and female employees?

a. Write down the regression equation using either the MINITAB or the Excel output and interpret the meaning of the regression equation.

b. Is there a difference, on the average, between the salaries of male and female employees? Test appropriate hypothesis to answer this question. Use a 5% level of significance.

Table 7.7 MINITAB output for the data in Table 7.6

```
Regression analysis: Salary (y) versus Yrs. of education, Yrs of
exp(x,..
The regression equation is
Salary (y) = 19.3 + 1.93 Yrs of education (x₁) + 1.62 Yrs of exp(x₂)
             + 1.78 Male (x₃)


Predictor               Coef   SE Coef      T      P
Constant              19.280     2.216   8.70  0.000
Yrs of education (x₁)  1.9273    0.2078   9.27  0.000
Yrs of exp(x₂)         1.6180    0.2328   6.95  0.000
Male (x₃)             1.7769    0.8346   2.13  0.043


S = 2.17582   R-Sq = 93.2%   R-Sq(adj) = 92.4%


Analysis of Variance


Source          DF      SS      MS      F      P
Regression       3  1675.58  558.53  117.98  0.000
Residual error  26   123.09    4.73
Total           29  1798.67
```

Table 7.8 Excel output for the data in Table 7.6

SUMMARY OUTPUT

Regression Statistics	
Multiple R	0.96518
R Square	0.93157
Adjusted R Square	0.92367
Standard Error	2.17582
Observations	30

ANOVA

	df	SS	MS	F	Significance F
Regression	3	1875.577	558.526	117.977	0.000
Residual	26	123.089	4.734		
Total	29	1798.667			

	Coefficients	Standard Erro	t Stat	P-value	Lower 95%	Upper 95%	Lower 95.0%	Upper 95.0%
Intercept	19.2798	2.2159	8.7007	0.0000	14.7250	23.8347	14.7250	23.8347
Yrs.Education (x1)	1.9273	0.2078	9.2734	0.0000	1.5001	2.3545	1.5001	2.3545
Yrs of Exp(x2)	1.6180	0.2328	6.9518	0.0000	1.1396	2.0965	1.1396	2.0965
Male (x3)	1.7769	0.8346	2.1291	0.0429	0.0614	3.4925	0.0614	3.4925

c. What salary would you predict for males with 12 years of education and 5 years of experience? What salary would you predict for females for the same years of education and work experience?

Solution:

a. The regression equation is shown in the MINITAB output (Table 7.7). The regression equation can also be written using the "coefficients" column of Excel output. The regression equation is

Salary (y) = 19.3 + 1.93 Yrs of education (x_1) + 1.62 Yrs of exp (x_2) + 1.78 Male (x_3) or,

$$\hat{y} = 19.3 + 1.93x_1 + 1.62x_2 + 1.78x_3 \qquad (7.1)$$

Note that the regression equation is of the form:

$$y = b_0 + b_1x_1 + b_2x_2 + b_3x_3$$

where x_3 is a dummy or indicator variable coded as "1" if the employee is a male or "0" if the employee is a female. It follows that we can write two separate equations: one for the male and other for the female employees.

For the **male employees**, $x_3 = 1$ and the relationship between the salary and the other indicator variables will take the following form:

$$y = b_0 + b_1x_1 + b_2x_2 + b_3(1)$$

or,

$$y = (b_0 + b_3) + b_1x_1 + b_2x_2$$

For the **female employees**, $x_3 = 0$ and the relationship between the salary and the other indicator variables will take the following form:

$$y = b_0 + b_1x_1 + b_2x_2 + b_3(0)$$

or,

$$y = b_0 + b_1x_1 + b_2x_2$$

The preceding are the two separate equations for the male and female employees. The regression equation (Equation 7.1) can be interpreted in the following ways:

- For each unit increase in the education or each additional year of education the salary increases by 1.93 (or 1.93 × 1,000 = $1930).
- For each year of experience obtained, the salary increases by 1.62 (or 1.62 × 1,000 = $1,620).
- Male employees earn, on average 1.78 or $1,780 more (or 1.78 × 1,000 = $1,780) per year than their female counterparts.

b. From the analysis of regression equation in part(a) we know that the males on the average earn $1,780 more than the females. We would like to know whether this amount is large enough to be considered statistically significant or this difference is purely by chance. To determine this, we need to test the coefficient of the indicator variable. This hypotheses can be written as:

$H_0 : \beta_3 = 0$ (No significant difference in average salary)

$H_1 : \beta_3 \neq 0$ (There is a significant difference in salary)

Thus, if the null hypothesis is not rejected, we conclude that there is no significant difference in the average salaries between male and female employees. On the other hand, if the null hypothesis is rejected, the difference is significant and the difference is not merely due to chance.

The previous hypothesis can be tested using the "p" column in either MINITAB or Excel computer results (Table 7.7 or 7.8). The decision rule for the p-value approach is given by:

If $p \geq \alpha$, do not reject H_0

If $p < \alpha$, reject H_0

From the tables, the p-value for the indicator variable male (x_3) is 0.0429 or

$$p = 0.0429$$

Since $p = 0.0429$ is less than $\alpha = 0.05$, we reject H_0 and conclude that there is a significant difference between the salaries of male and female employees, and males on the average earn significantly more than the females.

(a) The prediction equation:

$$\hat{y} = 19.3 + 1.93x_1 + 1.62x_2 + 1.78x_3$$

The prediction of average salary for males with 12 years of education and 5 years of work experience is:

$$x_1 = 12, x_2 = 5 \text{ and } x_3 = 1$$

$$\hat{y} = 19.3 + 1.93(12) + 1.62(5) + 1.78(1) = 52.34$$

or $52,340.

The corresponding average salary for females can be predicted as:

$$x_1 = 12, x_2 = 5, \text{ and } x_3 = 0$$

$$y = 19.3 + 1.93(12) + 1.62(5) + 1.78(0) = 50.56$$

or $50,560.

Interaction Models

In the regression models discussed earlier, it was assumed that the effect that an independent variable has on the dependent variable is independent of the other independent variables in the model. Sometimes, there may be an interaction between the independent variables. In such cases, the interaction between two independent variables means that the relationship between the dependent variable y and one independent variable x depends on the other x. For example, consider a regression model where we want to investigate the relationship between the profit of large retail stores and two independent variables: store location and store size. In this case, it is possible for the store location to have a large effect on the profit when the store size is large. On the other hand, if the store location is at a remote area, even the large stores may not change the profit significantly. In this case, store location and store size are said to interact and we can say that the effect that the store location has on the sale also depends on the size of the store. An interaction term can be used in this model to include the interaction effect. This interaction term is also known as a cross-product term.

An interaction model relating y and two quantitative independent variables can be written as:

$$y = b_0 + b_1 x_1 + b_2 x_2 + b_3 x_1 x_2 \qquad (7.2)$$

where $(b_1 + b_3 x_2)$ represents the change in y for every 1-unit increase in x_1 when x_2 is held constant, and $(b_2 + b_3 x_1)$ represents the change in y for every 1-unit increase in x_2 when x_1 is held constant.

Note that the interaction effect may occur between quantitative independent variables and also between a quantitative and a dummy variable.

Example 7.3: Regression Model with No Interaction

Suppose in a model, the response or the dependent variable y is related to two quantitative independent variables x_1 and x_2 by the first-order model:

$$y = 6 + 3x_1 + x_2$$

where $b_0 = 6$, $b_1 = 3$, and $b_2 = 1$.

In the preceding model, when $x_2 = 0$, the relationship between y and x_1 is given by:

$$y = 6 + 3x_1 + (0) = 6 + 3x_1$$

When $x_2 = 1$ and $x_2 = 2$, the relationships between y and x_1 can be given by:

$$y = 6 + 3x_1 + x_2 = 6 + 3x_1 + 1 = 7 + 3x_1$$

$$y = 6 + 3x_1 + x_2 = 6 + 3x_1 + 2 = 8 + 3x_1$$

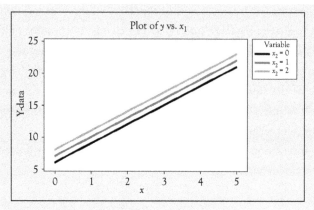

Figure 7.4 *Graph* $y = 6 + 3x_1 + x_2$ *for* $x_2 = 0,1,2$

A graph of these relationships is shown in Figure 7.4. Note that the slopes of all these lines are equal to 3 and hence these lines are parallel. This figure shows an important characteristic of the first-order model. If we graph the equation of the type:

$$y = 6 + 3x_1 + x_2$$

for one variable x_1 while keeping the value of other variable fixed, the result will always be a straight line with slope equal to b_1. If we plot this equation for other values of fixed independent variables, we will obtain a set of parallel lines as shown in Figure 7.4.

This indicates that the effect of independent variable x_i on the dependent variable y is independent of all the other independent variables, or in other words, the relationship between y and any independent variable does not depend on the values of other independent variables. This also shows that there is no interaction among the independent variables.

Example 7.4: Regression Model with Interaction

Suppose in a model, the response of the dependent variable y is related to two quantitative independent variables, x_1 and x_2 by the model:

$$y = 3 + 5x_1 - x_2 + 4x_1x_2$$

A graph of y and x_1 for $x_2 = 0$, 1, and 2 is shown in Figure 7.5.

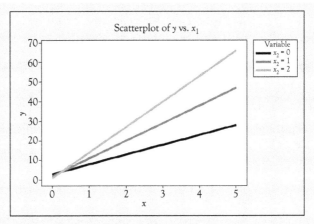

Figure 7.5 Graph of $y = 3 + 5x_1 - x_2 + 4x_1x_2$

The plot in Figure 7.5 shows three nonparallel straight lines indicating that the slopes of the lines differ. The slopes of the lines can be determined by substitution of the different values of $x_2 = 0$, 1, and 2 as shown in the following.

For $x_2 = 0$:

$$y = 3 + 5x_1 - x_2 + 4x_1x_2 = 3 + 5x_1 - 0 + 4x_1(0) = 3 + 5x_1$$

For $x_2 = 1$:

$$y = 3 + 5x_1 - x_2 + 4x_1x_2 = 3 + 5x_1 - 1 + 4x_1(1) = 2 + 9x_1$$

For $x_2 = 2$:

$$y = 3 + 5x_1 - x_2 + 4x_1x_2 = 3 + 5x_1 - 2 + 4x_1(2) = 1 + 13x_1$$

The preceding shows that the effect on y of a change in x_1 (or the slope) depends on the value of x_2. This means that x_1 and x_2 interact or have an interaction effect. The term $x_1.x_2$, which is a cross-product term, is known as an interaction term and the model:

$$y = b_0 + b_1x_1 + b_2x_2 + b_3x_1x_2$$

is an interaction model.

Example 7.5: Interaction Model

The data file **MPG-INTERACTION.MTW** and **MPG-INTER-ACTION.xlsx** contains the variables shown in the following. We would like to predict the fuel consumption in miles per gallon (Mpg) using the independent variables. Since we are trying to predict the fuel consumption, this variable is the dependent or response variable. The variables involved in the model and their units of measurements are described as follows.

y = miles per gallon (Mpg)
x_1 = average speed of the car in miles per hour (Av. speed)
x_2 = Weight of the automobile (in thousands of pounds)
x_3 = Horsepower
x_4 = Altitude (in thousands of feet)

a. Using MINITAB or Excel, develop a regression model that includes x_1, x_2, x_3, and x_4. Show the computer results of MINITAB or Excel.

b. Using MINITAB or Excel, develop a regression model that includes x_1, x_2, x_3, x_4, and the interaction of x_2 and x_3 (interaction of weight and horsepower, $x_2 * x_3$). Show the computer results of MINITAB or Excel.

c. At a 5% level of significance, is there evidence that the interaction term makes a significant contribution in predicting y?

d. Which regression model: the model in part (a) or (b) should be used to predict the miles per gallon (y)?

Solution:

a. The MINITAB regression output is shown in Table 7.9.

b. The interaction model using Excel is shown in Table 7.10.

c. To test whether the interaction is significant, we test the null hypothesis

$$H_0 : \beta_5 = 0$$
$$H_1 : \beta_5 \neq 0$$

Table 7.9 Regression output for Mpg (y) and four independent variables

```
Regression analysis: Mpg (y) versus Av. speed (x₁), Weight (x₂),
...

The regression equation is
Mpg (y) = 12.3 + 0.299 Av. speed (x₁) - 2.51 Weight (x₂) + 0.0939
          Horsepower (x₃) - 2.08 Altitude (x₄)


Predictor            Coef  SE Coef        T       P
Constant           12.290    5.552     2.21   0.039
Av. speed (x₁)    0.29858  0.03742     7.98   0.000
Weight (x₂)       -2.5060   0.6909    -3.63   0.002
Horsepower (x₃)   0.09386  0.02804     3.35   0.003
Altitude (x₄)     -2.0763   0.3027    -6.86   0.000


S = 1.45399    R-Sq = 93.2%   R-Sq(adj) = 91.9%


Analysis of Variance


Source          DF      SS       MS      F       P
Regression       4  581.16   145.29  68.72   0.000
Residual error  20   42.28     2.11
Total           24  623.44
```

Table 7.10 Interaction model using Excel

SUMMARY OUTPUT

Regression Statistics	
Multiple R	0.98008
R Square	0.96056
Adjusted R Square	0.95018
Standard Error	1.13759
Observations	25

ANOVA

	df	SS	MS	F	Significance F
Regression	5	598.8520	119.7704	92.5508	0.0000
Residual	19	24.5880	1.2941		
Total	24	623.4400			

	Coefficients	Standard Error	t Stat	P-value	Lower 95%	Upper 95%	Lower 95.0%	Upper 95.0%
Intercept	-59.7475	19.9602	-2.9933	0.0075	-101.5248	-17.9703	-101.5248	-17.9703
Av.Speed (x1)	0.2628	0.0308	8.5228	0.0000	0.1983	0.3273	0.1983	0.3273
Weight (x2)	13.2519	4.2958	3.0849	0.0061	4.2608	22.2430	4.2608	22.2430
Horsepower (x3)	0.6632	0.1555	4.2642	0.0004	0.3377	0.9887	0.3377	0.9887
Altitude (x4)	-2.1624	0.2380	-9.0866	0.0000	-2.6605	-1.6643	-2.6605	-1.6643
Weight * Horsepower (x2*x3)	-0.1226	0.0332	-3.6977	0.0015	-0.1920	-0.0532	-0.1920	-0.0532

The null hypothesis means that the interaction—weight*horsepower$(x_2 * x_3)$ is not significant, whereas the alternate hypothesis means that the interaction is significant.

The previous hypothesis can be tested using the p-value approach. From the computer output in Table 7.10, the p-value for the interaction term, weight*horsepower($x_2 * x_3$) is 0.0015. At $\alpha = 0.05$, we see that p is less than 0.05 (or, $p = 0.0015 < \alpha = 0.05$); therefore, we reject the null hypothesis and conclude that the interaction is significant.

d. The interaction model in part (b) should be used to predict the miles per gallon (y). Note that the r^2 and also the standard error of the estimate (s) both improved for the interaction model (compare the results in Tables 7.9 and 7.10).

Example 7.6: Another Example on Interaction Model

The general manager of a chain of stores hired a consultant to develop a model to learn whether there is a relationship between the sales of the chain's three stores located in different areas of a small town. The manager would like to predict the sales of one of its larger store using the sales of the other two stores. The consultant decided to build a multiple regression model relating the sales of three stores. He used the sales of store 2 and 3 to predict the sales for store 1. Table 7.11 shows the sales for three stores.

Sales—Store 1 (y)
Sales—Store 2, x_1 (×100)
Sales—Store 3, x_2 (×100)

The data files: *STORE SALES.MTW* and **STORE SALES.xlsx** show the MINITAB and Excel data files for this problem.

a. Using MINITAB or Excel, develop a regression model that includes x_1 and x_2 to predict the sales for store 1. Show the computer results of MINITAB or Excel.

b. Using MINITAB or Excel, develop a regression model that includes x_1 and x_2 and the interaction of x_1 and x_2 (interaction of store 1 and store 2 sales) to predict the sales for store 1. Show the computer results of MINITAB or Excel.

c. At a 5% level of significance, is there evidence that the interaction term makes a significant contribution in predicting the sales y?

Table 7.11 Sales of three stores

Row	Sales-Store 1 (y)	Sales-Store 2 (x_1)	Sales-Store 3 (x_2)
1	82	72	70
2	78	72	70
3	76	76	64
4	90	102	82
5	92	104	78
6	86	110	110
7	94	114	104
8	88	106	108
9	82	124	130
10	70	140	154
11	72	144	150
12	78	148	148
13	66	166	162
14	66	166	162
15	56	202	184
16	62	214	182

d. Comment on the regression models in part (a) and (b).

Solution:

a. The MINITAB computer output with the prediction equation is shown in Table 7.12.

b. The interaction model using MINITAB is shown in Table 7.13. Note that the interaction model is of the form:

$$y = b_0 + b_1 x_1 + b_2 x_2 + b_3 x_1 x_2$$

c. To test whether the interaction is significant, we test the null hypotheses:

$$H_0 : \beta_3 = 0$$
$$H_1 : \beta_3 \neq 0$$

Table 7.12 MINITAB regression output

```
Regression analysis: Sales-Store (1) versus Sales-Store (2), Sales-Store (3)


The regression equation is
Sales-Store 1(y) = 103 - 0.069 Sales-Store 2 (x₁) - 0.138
                        Sales-Store 3 (x₂)


Predictor                Coef  SE Coef       T      P
Constant              103.109    6.379   16.16  0.000
Sales-Store 2 (x₁)    -0.0686    0.1626  -0.42  0.680
Sales-Store 3 (x₂)    -0.1381    0.1676  -0.82  0.425


S = 7.83825   R-Sq = 58.4%   R-Sq(adj) = 51.9%


Analysis of Variance


Source            DF       SS      MS      F      P
Regression         2  1119.05  559.53   9.11  0.003
Residual error    13   798.70   61.44
Total             15  1917.75
```

Table 7.13 Interaction model using MINITAB

```
Regression analysis: Sales-Store (1) versus Sales-Store (2), Sales-Store (3), and
interaction ....
The regression equation is
Sales-Store 1(y) = 23.8 + 0.973 Sales-Store 2 (x₁) + 0.143 Sales-
Store 3 (x₂) - 0.00514 x₁ * x₂
Predictor                Coef     SE Coef       T      P
Constant               23.82       12.64    1.88  0.084
Sales-Store 2 (x₁)      0.9730      0.1796   5.42  0.000
Sales-Store 3 (x₂)      0.14332     0.09307  1.54  0.150
x₁ * x₂                -0.0051393   0.0007939 -6.47  0.000


S = 3.84941   R-Sq = 90.7%   R-Sq(adj) = 88.4%


Analysis of Variance


Source            DF       SS      MS      F      P
Regression         3  1739.93  579.98  39.14  0.000
Residual error    12   177.82   14.82
Total             15  1917.75
```

The null hypothesis means that the interaction is not significant, whereas the alternate hypothesis means that the interaction is significant.

The preceding hypotheses can be tested using the p-value approach. From the computer output in Table 7.13, the p-value for the interaction term $(x_1 * x_2)$ is 0.000. At $\alpha = 0.05$, we see that p is less than 0.05 (or, $p = 0.000 < \alpha = 0.05$); therefore, we reject the null hypothesis and conclude that the interaction is significant.

d. The regression model in part (a)—the model without the interaction term in Table 7.12 shows that both the independent variables are insignificant at a 5% level of significance (the p-values for x_1 and x_2 are 0.680 and 0.425). This model also has a low r^2 value of 58.4%. However, the overall model is significant as can be seen from the *Analysis of Variance* part of the computer output in Table 7.12, which shows an F-value of 9.11 with a corresponding p-value of 0.003. At $\alpha = 0.05$, we see that p is less than 0.05 (or $p = 0.003 < \alpha = 0.05$); therefore, we can conclude that the overall model is statistically significant.

Table 7.13 shows the interaction model with independent variables x_1 and x_2 and the interaction term $x_1 x_2$. This model shows a significant improvement both in the value of r^2 and the standard error of the estimate (s). The r^2 in this model is 90.7% compared to 58.4% in the model of part (a). The standard error of the estimate (s) also dropped to 3.849 compared to 7.838 in the model without interaction in part (a). Overall, there is a significant improvement in the model because of the inclusion of the interaction term.

It is important to investigate the effect of interaction terms in the model because the effect of the independent variables sometimes is not additive because of interacting effects between the variables. In such cases, the inclusion of interaction terms may significantly improve the model. The other important point to note here is that once it is determined that the interaction is significant in the model:

$$y = b_0 + b_1 x_1 + b_2 x_2 + b_3 x_1 x_2$$

it is not necessary to conduct t-tests on the individual b_i coefficients of the first-order terms x_1 and x_2 as these terms should be retained in the model regardless of their p-values once the interaction term $x_1 x_2$ has been deemed significant.

Finding the Best Possible Prediction Equation Using Regression

In a data set involving several variables, there is generally one response variable y whose value we want to predict using several independent variables. In doing so we often ask the question which variables are significant or which independent variables should be included in the model, and which ones should be discarded. In course of finding the best prediction equation, we would like to achieve the following:

- Find a regression line, a plane, or a hyperplane that explains a high percentage of variability in y. The appropriate measure for this purpose is the coefficient of determination r^2.
- Keep the regression equation simple. This can be done by minimizing the number of independent variables or predictors in the model.

The previous two goals are contradictory. The amount of unexplained variation can be increased by adding more predictors or independent variables to the model and this can make the model more complex. Therefore, some trade-off must be made between getting a high r^2 and finding a suitable number of independent variables. The following section shows how to search for the best predictors.

All Subset Regression

Suppose we have m independent variables in a regression model. All these predictors may not be significant; that is, all m predictors may not be needed to obtain the best predictor equation. Our objective is to find the best predictors. To achieve this we may have to perform all possible sets of regression. In general, if there are m independent variables, we have:

$$2^m - 1$$

predictor set, each having a distinct regression equation. Thus, in a data set containing three predictors or independent variable, there are:

$$2^3 - 1 = 7$$

possible regressions. This is explained with an example. Suppose we want to predict the fuel consumption in miles per gallon (y) for a particular size of automobile and would like to relate the response y to three predictors, average speed of the automobile, weight of the car in thousands of pounds, and the horsepower. That is,

y = miles per gallon (mpg) x_1 = average speed
x_2 = weight x_3 = horsepower

The all possible subset regression for the preceding problem would contain seven regression equations. These are shown in Table 7.14. If

Table 7.14 *All possible regressions for three predictors*

Predictor set	Regression equation	Coefficient of determination (r^2) (%)
x_1	Mpg (y) = 7.37 + 0.324 Av. speed (x_1)	R-Sq = 25.6
x_2	Mpg (y) = 46.9 – 5.64 Weight (x_2)	R-Sq = 40.9
x_3	Mpg (y) = –11.0 + 0.261 Horsepower (x_3)	R-Sq = 54.5
x_1, x_2	Mpg (y) = 30.7 + 0.307 Av. speed (x_1) – 5.46 Weight (x_2)	R-Sq = 63.8
x_1, x_3	Mpg (y) = –18.8 + 0.230 Av. speed (x_1) + 0.233 Horsepower (x_3)	R-Sq = 66.7
x_2, x_3	Mpg (y) = 8.6 – 2.66 Weight (x_2) + 0.196 Horsepower (x_3)	R-Sq = 60.2
x_1, x_2, x_3	Mpg (y) = 3.8 + 0.253 Av. speed (x_1) – 3.17 Weight (x_2) + 0.152 Horsepower (x_3)	R-Sq = 74.7

there are 4 predictors, there would be 15 predictor sets and 15 distinct regression equations. Similarly, the number of possible regressions for 10 predictors or independent variables would be:

$$2^{10} - 1 = 1023$$

Thus, if we want to perform all possible regressions on a set of data having several predictors, it would be a tremendous amount of work and the process would not be efficient. There is another procedure that is often used in cases where several predictors are involved. This procedure minimizes the computational effort and is known as **stepwise regression**.

Stepwise Regression

Stepwise regression is often used to select the independent variables in a regression model that may have a large set of independent variables. In many regression problems the list of potentially important independent variables may be extremely long and it may be difficult to select the variables to include in the model. For example, in predicting sales, the independent variables may include the advertisement cost, bonus paid, number of sales persons, the regions where the marketing efforts are diverted, and so on. Similarly, in determining which variables affect the profit of a firm, such as blood sugar level of patients, salary of the executives, and fuel consumption of automobiles, the list of potential independent variables may be extremely long. Building an effective regression model with a large number of independent variables is a common regression problem and is also challenging. The problem becomes more complex if higher order terms and interactions are needed in the model. Stepwise regression is helpful in such cases. It is a screening process that helps to determine which of the large set of independent variables to include in the model.

In the stepwise regression procedure, the response variable y and a set of potentially important independent variables, $x_1, x_2, x_3, x_4, \ldots, x_k$ are identified. The independent variables may include first-order or higher order terms and also dummy variables. In our example, we will only consider the first-order terms. Often a computer software is used to run the stepwise regression model. Once the data including the response and the independent variables are submitted to the software, the stepwise regression procedure works as described in Table 7.15.

Table 7.15 Stepwise regression steps

Step 1: The software program first fits the regression model with all possible variables, one variable at a time. This model is of the form

$$y = b_0 + b_1 x_i$$

where x_i are the independent variables with $i = 1, 2, 3, ..., k$.
Next, the following hypotheses are tested using the t-test or the equivalent F-test for each model:

$$H_0 : \beta_1 = 0$$
$$H_1 : \beta_1 \neq 0$$

The independent variable with the largest t-value (in absolute term) is considered the best one-variable predictor and is the first one to be included in the model.

Step 2: In this step, the software program searches for the second variable from the remaining $(k-1)$ variables to be included in the model. This is done to determine the best two variables to be included in the model. The second model contains the x_1 variable determined in the first step and the second variable determined from the remaining $(k-1)$ variables and is of the form:

$$y = b_0 + b_1 x_1 + b_2 x_i$$

Then the hypotheses $H_0 : \beta_2 = 0$ versus $H_1 : \beta_2 \neq 0$ are tested for each of the $(k-1)$ variables to search for the second variable. The t-values for the tests are computed for each of the variables, where, $i = 1, 2, 3, ..., k$ and the variable with the largest t is selected as the second variable to be included in the model.

At this point, the stepwise regression works like backward elimination procedure. This means that after adding a new variable to the model, the procedure retests the t-value of b_1 after $b_2 x_2$ has been added to the model. If it finds that the t-value has become insignificant at some specified α level (say $\alpha = 0.15$), then x_1 is removed from the model and a new search is made for an independent variable that provides the most significant t-value to be included in the model.

The reason the t-value for x_1 may change after including the second variable in Step 2 is that the inclusion of second variable results in a response surface with a plane and the equation of a best fitting plane may yield a different value for b_1 than what was obtained in Step 1. For this reason, the software packages that recheck the t-values at each step should be used for stepwise procedure.

Step 3: In the third step, the software program searches for a third variable from the remaining $(k-2)$ variables to be included in the model to determine the third variable for the model with x_1 and x_2 in the model. That is, we search the best model of the form

$$y = b_0 + b_1 x_1 + b_2 x_2 + b_3 x_i$$

To obtain the third best variable to be included in the model, the software fits the models using x_1, x_2 and each of the remaining $(k-2)$ variables, x_i and finds the best third variable x_3.

After adding a new variable at each step, the software program retests the coefficients of previously added variables and removes the variables with t-values that have become nonsignificant. Once no further variables are found that yield significant t-values at a specified α level, the procedure terminates.

NOTE: The stepwise procedure uses an extremely large number of t-tests (depending on the number of independent variables). This may lead to a high probability of type I or type II error. When a large number of t-tests are conducted on the regression coefficients, the probability may be very high that some unimportant independent variables are included in the model (Type I errors) or some important variables are excluded (Type II errors).

Example 7.7—Stepwise Regression

For the stepwise regression example, we will use the data shown in Table 7.16. In this problem the fuel consumption of automobiles in miles per gallon (Mpg) is related to five independent variables or predictors. We will use MINITAB to run a stepwise regression model to screen out the nonsignificant variables and build a regression model. The data are in file **MULTIREG (MPG). MTW.**

The stepwise regression output is shown in Table 7.17 followed by an analysis of the computer results. The steps to run the stepwise regression using MINITAB are explained in *Appendix A_Table A.17.*

Note that in Table 7.17, the first variable included in the model is x_3 (horsepower). The next variable to be included in the model is

Table 7.16 Fuel consumption (Mpg)

Row	Mpg (y)	Av.speed (x_1)	Weight (x_2)	Horsepower (x_3)	Altitude (x_4)	P weight (x_5)
1	18	40	4.2	120	3	5
2	22	37	3.8	135	2	3
3	31	60	4.0	140	1	4
4	25	50	3.9	132	2	3
5	30	51	4.2	142	1	4
6	21	44	3.0	130	3	5
7	29	45	3.8	142	1	3
8	32	64	3.2	148	3	2
9	15	46	4.8	96	4	5
10	20	45	4.5	130	2	3
11	23	57	4.2	138	3	3
12	32	57	3.4	140	1	1
13	22	38	4.1	141	3	2
14	24	40	4.0	142	2	3
15	17	52	5.5	100	4	5
16	20	48	4.3	110	2	2
17	23	40	4.1	142	2	3
18	25	56	3.8	135	3	4
19	15	52	5.5	110	5	5
20	26	60	4.5	148	3	3
21	26	52	3.8	138	3	3
22	30	62	3.7	135	3	5
23	22	48	4.0	140	4	3
24	26	60	4.4	148	3	4
25	18	53	4.3	136	5	4

Table 7.17 MINITAB output for stepwise regression

```
Stepwise regression: Mpg (y) versus Av. speed (x₁), Weight (x₂), ...

Alpha-to-Enter: 0.15  Alpha-to-Remove: 0.15

Response is Mpg (y) on 5 predictors, with N = 25


Step                    1       2       3       4
Constant          -10.965   2.669  -4.099   7.409


Horsepower (x₃)     0.261   0.198   0.145   0.107
T-value              5.24    4.37    5.16    3.66
P-value             0.000   0.000   0.000   0.002


Altitude (x₄)               -1.94   -2.43   -2.20
T-value                     -3.37   -6.96   -6.78
P-value                     0.003   0.000   0.000


Av. speed (x₁)                      0.301   0.307
T-value                              6.45    7.35
P-value                             0.000   0.000


Weight (x₂)                                 -1.80
T-value                                     -2.49
P-value                                     0.021


S                    3.51    2.92    1.73    1.55
R-Sq                54.46   70.00   89.94   92.33
R-Sq(adj)           52.48   67.27   88.50   90.79
Mallows Cp           92.1    55.5     8.0     4.0
```

Altitude (x_4) in Step 2. In Steps 3 and 4, the variables to be included in the model are x_1 (Average speed) and x_2 (the weight). After Step 4, MINITAB stops because no other variables met the criterion for inclusion into the model. Note that MINITAB uses $\alpha = 0.15$ for the t-tests. This means that if the p-value associated with a regression coefficient (b) exceeds $\alpha = 0.15$, the variable is not included in the model.

The computer results using the stepwise regression in MINITAB suggest that we should include the four independent variables x_3, x_4,

x_1, and x_2 in the model. Based on the result of the stepwise regression in Table 7.17, the best model appears to be:

$$Mpg\ (y) = 7.409 + 0.307\ Av.\ speed\ (x_1) - 1.80\ Weight\ (x_2)$$
$$+ 0.107\ Horsepower\ (x_3) - 2.20\ Altitude\ (x_4)$$

The previous model is written using the column labeled (4) in the stepwise regression output in Table 7.17. At this point, models with interactions and second-order terms should be evaluated to determine the best possible model for predicting the fuel consumption y or Mpg.

Another Look at Stepwise Regression

In building the regression model, often we want to find the model that explains a high percentage of variability in y. The appropriate measure for this purpose is the coefficient of determination r^2. Refer to the row that displays the coefficient of multiple determination "R-sq" in Table 7.17. Figure 7.6(a) and (b) display decision trees that show how the independent variables are added in a stepwise regression based on the value of r^2.

In Figure 7.6(a), regression is performed with each of the independent variables. The coefficient of determination with each independent variable is shown in this figure. The largest coefficient of determination r^2 is 54.5% for the third variable x_3 (horsepower). Therefore, this is the first predictor variable added to the model. The decision tree shows that the variable x_3 with a r^2 value of 54.5% is the first one to be included in the model.

In the second step, the regression is performed with y, the response variable x_3 (the variable selected in Step 1), and the remaining independent variables added one at a time. The r^2 values with each of independent variables are shown in Figure 7.6(a). The largest r^2 is obtained by adding the predictor x_4 to the model. This value is shown as $R^2yx_3x_4 = 70.0\%$ and also in Step 2 of Table 7.17. This is the next predictor to be included in the model.

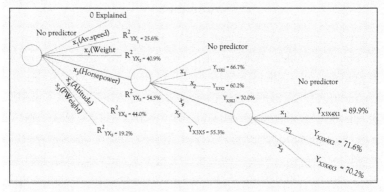

Figure 7.6(a) Decision tree for adding predictors in stepwise regression

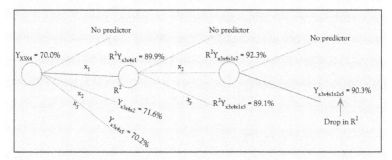

Figure 7.6(b) Decision tree for adding predictors in stepwise regression and the prediction equation

The steps are continued in Figure 7.6(b). The process continues in the same way and is usually terminated when there is no improvement in the r^2 value by adding other predictor to the model. Note that in each step of the decision tree in Figure 7.6(a) and (b), there is a branch indicating "No predictor." This simply means that we may choose not to add any predictor to be included in the model.

The prediction equation based on the decision-tree model:

$$\text{Mpg } (y) = 7.41 + 0.307 \text{ Av. speed } (x_1) - 1.80 \text{ Weight } (x_2)$$
$$+ 0.107 \text{ Horsepower } (x_3) - 2.20 \text{ Altitude } (x_4)$$

Summary

In this chapter, we discussed models other than the multiple and quadratic or nonlinear models. In particular, we explored the following models: (a) models with qualitative independent (dummy) variables, (b) interaction models, (c) all subset regression, and (d) stepwise regression models. The dummy variables are the qualitative variables that are often required to be included in the regression model. The example of dummy variables would be the sales territories where a company operates. To include different zones or the territories in predicting the sales for a company, the dummy variables could be included in a regression model. In this chapter, we presented examples of dummy variables and provided computer analysis of these models. The other regression model we discussed is known as the interaction model. This type of model takes into account the effect of interaction between the independent variables. We presented a regression model that investigated the relationship between the profit of large retail stores and two independent variables store location and store size. We demonstrated that the profit of the stores under investigation depends not only on the store size and location of stores but a combination of these two variables—the store size and location also influences the profit. This required an interaction term to be added to the model. In many cases, there may be an interaction among the variables. Adding an interaction term can greatly improve the predicting ability of the model.

We also introduced the concept of *All Subset Regression*. In building a regression model, often the objective is to determine the model that explains a high percentage of variability in the response variable y. This is measured using the coefficient of determination r^2. The all subset regression method can be used to search for the best predictors to be included in the model. Finally, we discussed *Stepwise Regression* method. This method is often used to select the independent variables or predictors from a large set of independent variables in the model. A computer example was presented to demonstrate the procedure of identifying potentially important independent variables to be included in the model.

CHAPTER 8

Notes on Implementation of Regression Models

Regression Models

Regression is a powerful tool and is widely used in studying the relationships among the variables. A number of regression models were discussed in this book. These models are summarized here:

Simple linear regression	$y = \beta_0 + \beta_1 x + \varepsilon$
Multiple regression	$y = \beta_0 + \beta_1 x_1 + \beta_2 x_2 + \ldots + \beta_k x_k + \varepsilon$
Polynomial regression (second-order models can be extended to higher order model)	Second-order polynomial: $y = \beta_0 + \beta_1 x_1 + \beta_2 x_2^2 + \varepsilon$ Higher order polynomial: $y = \beta_0 + \beta_1 x_1 + \beta_2 x_2^2 + \ldots + \beta_k x_k^k + \varepsilon$
Interaction models	An interaction model relating y and two quantitative independent variables can be written as $y = b_0 + b_1 x_1 + b_2 x_2 + b_3 x_1 x_2$
Models with dummy variables	General form of model with one qualitative (dummy) independent variable at m levels $y = b_0 + b_1 x_1 + b_2 x_2 + \ldots + b_{m-1} x_{m-1}$ where x_i is the dummy variable for level $(i + 1)$ and $x_i = \begin{cases} 1 & \text{if } y \text{ is observed at level } (i+1) \\ 0 & \text{otherwise} \end{cases}$
All subset and stepwise regression	Finding the best set of predictor variables to be included in the model

There are other regression models that are not discussed here. Other models can be developed using the concepts presented. Some of these models are explained here.

Reciprocal transformation of x variable	This transformation can produce a linear relationship and is of the form: $y = \beta_0 + \beta_1\left(\dfrac{1}{x}\right) + \varepsilon$ This model is appropriate when x and y have an inverse relationship. Note that the inverse relationship is not linear.
Log transformation of x variable	The logarithmic transformation is of the form: $y = \beta_0 + \beta_1 \ln(x) + \varepsilon$ This is a useful curvilinear form where $\ln(x)$ is the natural logarithm of x and $x > 0$.
Log transformation of x and y variables	$\ln(y) = \beta_0 + \beta_1 \ln(x) + \varepsilon$ The purpose of this transformation is to achieve a linear relationship. The model is valid for positive values of x and y. This transformation is more involved and is difficult to compare to the other models with y as the dependent variable.
Logistic regression	This model is used when the response variable is categorical. In all the regression models we developed in this book, response variable was a quantitative variable. In cases where the response is categorical or qualitative, the simple and multiple least squares regression model violates the normality assumption. The correct model in this case is logistic regression and is not discussed in this book.

Implementation Steps and Strategy for Regression Models

Successful implementation of regression models requires an understanding of different types of models. A knowledge of least squares method on which many of the regression models are based as well as the awareness of the assumptions of least squares regression are critical in evaluating and implementing the correct regression models. The computer packages have made the model building and analysis easy. As we have demonstrated, the scatterplots and matrix plots constructed using the computer are very helpful in the initial stages of selecting the right model for the given data. The residual plots for checking the assumptions of regression can be easily constructed using computer. While the computer packages have removed the computational hurdle, it is important to understand the fundamentals underlying the regression to use the regression models properly. A lack of understanding of least squares method and the assumptions underlying the regression may lead to drawing wrong conclusions and selecting incorrect alternative course of action. For example, if the assumptions of regression are violated, it is important to determine the alternate course or courses of action. The following are important considerations in regression and modeling.

Guidelines for Simple Linear Regression

- In case of simple regression, construct a scatterplot to identify the possible relationship between x and y.
- Construct a matrix plot to investigate the possible relationships between the response variable y and the independent variables.
- Compute and interpret the regression statistics including the standard error of the estimate, coefficient of determination (r^2), and adjusted-r^2.
- Construct the plots of residuals and check for the assumptions of regression. In case of linear regression, analyze the residual plots to check whether normality, equality of variance, and the independence of error assumptions are met.
- Check the plot of residuals versus the fitted values or fits to confirm that the selected linear or quadratic model is appropriate. Always perform residual analysis to check for the model adequacy.
- If data were collected over time, plot the residuals versus time and use the Durbin–Watson test to check for the independence or errors (check whether the errors are correlated).
- If the assumptions of regression are not met, consider alternative methods to least squares regression.
- If regression assumptions are met, carry out the tests for the significance of regression coefficients and develop confidence and prediction intervals.
- Test for outliers and influential observations.
- Make prediction using the fitted regression line. Avoid making predictions outside the relevant range of the independent variable. Figure 8.1 outlines these steps.

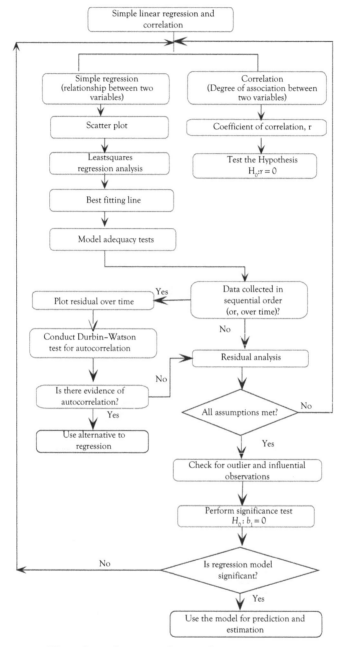

Figure 8.1 Flow chart depicting the simple regression steps

Guidelines for Multiple Regression and Modeling

The flow chart in Figure 8.2 provides guidelines and possible steps for building the multiple regression models. Many of these steps are similar to what we discussed earlier for the simple regression model and described in the flow chart of Figure 8.1. Some additional steps are needed for multiple regression models. These are outlined as follows:

- For multiple regression models, construct the matrix plot to identify the correct model.
- Decide whether the first-order model is adequate for the data, or the interaction or higher order terms should be included.
- Build the appropriate model and check for the model adequacy by evaluating the residual plots. Make sure that all the assumptions of the model are satisfied.
- If the interaction or higher order terms are included in the model, evaluate these terms.
- If all the assumptions of regression are satisfied, conduct the F-test for the overall significance of the model.
- Conduct the t-tests for the significance of each of the independent variables.
- Compute the variance inflation factor (VIF) for each independent variable to determine which ones to include in the model.
- Conduct the influence analysis and tests for outliers to determine whether to remove any observations from the model.
- Consider alternative models for the problem if necessary.
- Use all subset and stepwise regression models if a large number of variables are under consideration.

Summary

This chapter provided an overview of the models considered in this book. Two flow charts were presented outlining the steps to guide the user through the regression and modeling steps. The first flow chart described the steps that should be followed in building, constructing, and implementing the simple regression model. The second flow chart relates to

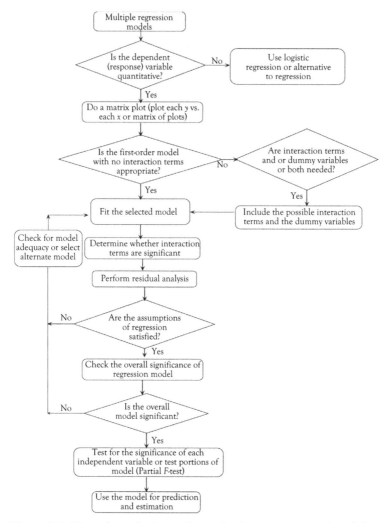

Figure 8.2 Flow chart depicting the multiple regression and modeling steps

the implementation steps for multiple regression, interaction, and other models. Model building is an art that can be mastered through practice. A number of models are at the disposal of the user and it is difficult to agree on the best multiple regression model. The strategies in this chapter are expected to avoid some of the pitfalls of multiple regression and modeling. Use of computers in building and implementing these models definitely relieves one from complex computations involved in these models.

Bibliography

Dielman, T. 2001. *Applied Regression Analysis for Business and Economics.* Belmont, CA: Brooks/Cole.

Kleinbaum, D., and L. Kupper. 1997. *Applied Regression Analysis and Other Multivariable Methods.* 2nd ed. Duxbury.

Mendenhall, W., and T.A. Sincich. 2003. *Second Course in Statistics: Regression Analysis.* 6th ed. Prentice Hall.

McClave, J.T., P.G. Benson, and T. Sincich. 2011. *Statistics for Business and Economics.* 11th ed. Pearson Education, Inc.

Montgomery, D., E. Peek, and G. Vining. 2011. *Introduction to Linear Regression Analysis.* 3rd ed. Wiley.

Savin, N.E., and K.J. White. 1977. "The Durbin-Watson Test for Serial Correlation with Extreme Sample Sizes or Many Regressors." *Econometrica: Journal of the Econometric Society* 45, no. 8, pp. 1989–96.

Index

CPSIA information can be obtained
at www.ICGtesting.com
Printed in the USA
LVHW080148311021
701984LV00006B/71

9 781631 573293